30th SEPTEMBER 2000

To John & Au
With all good
from
Frances & Ernie

Mary Victoria of Teck
By courtesy of the National Portrait Gallery, London.

Queen Mary's Hospital For Children

by

Ernest Earl

AN HISTORICAL ACCOUNT THROUGH WORDS & PICTURES

Queen Mary's Hospital for Children

First edition 1996
Second edition 1996
Third edition June 1996
Revised and Reprinted 1996

ISBN 0 907616 98 4

copyright© Ernest Earl

While every effort has been made to obtain copyright permission on published photographs and articles it may be that some material that may still be in copyright has been published inadvertently without permission. Should this have occurred then the author apologises.'

contact Ernest Earl
Tel: 01737-822661

All rights reserved. No part of this publication may be reproduced stored in a retrieval system or transmitted, in any form or by any means, electronic, mechanical, photocopying, recording or otherwise, without the prior permission of the publishers.

Published by
Able Publishing Services
13 Station Road, Knebworth,
Herts. SG3 6AP
Tel: 01438 814316 Fax: 01438 815232

Printing and photograph production
by Triographics, Knebworth, Herts.

CONTENTS

	page no.
Introduction	11
About the Author	15
Chapter 1 Queen Mary's Hospital for Children by Dr. Nicholas C Silva	17
Chapter 2 Patients section	35
Chapter 3 The Hospital School	59
Chapter 4 The Music Festival	93
Chapter 5 Let's Make A Game Of It	101
Chapter 6 The Late Joe Smith and Joe's Story	107
Chapter 7 Friend's of Queen Mary's Hospital for Children amd Orchard Hill	115
Chapter 8 Historic & Modern Photographs	121
Chapter 9 History and Archaeology.	165
Surrey Archaeological Society – Report on excavations at the site of the early iron camp in the grounds of Queen Mary's Hospital, Carshalton.	171
Chapter 10 Conclusion	193

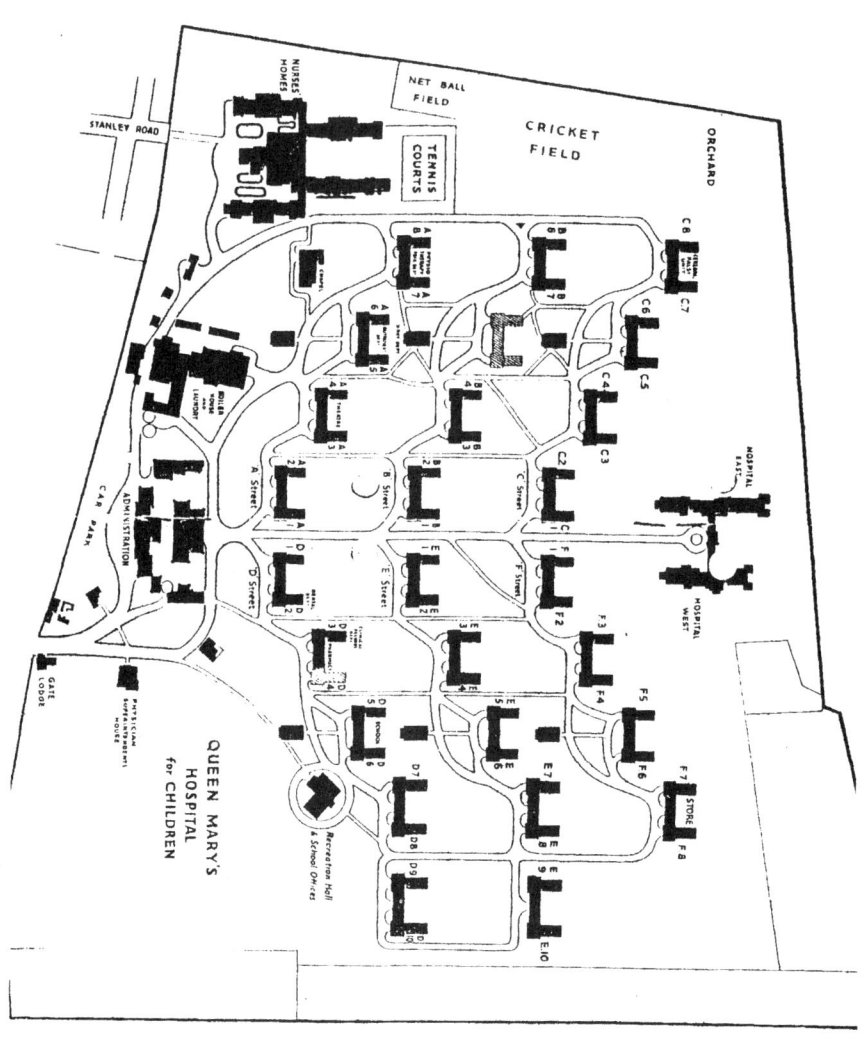

Queen Mary's Area Plan

A photograph of the Hospital, taken from the air, showing the six echelons of ward blocks. On the right in the background are the nurses' and staff homes.
The entrance to the Hospital is at the top left hand corner.
Reproduced by courtesy of Aerofilms Ltd.

PREFACE

This is a history of Queen Mary's Hospital for Children as I knew it on its original site in Carshalton. The excellent work which began in 1909 is being continued on its present site at the St. Helier NHS Trust Hospital, Carshalton.

This book is by no means a dry or concise history of Queen Mary's Hospital for Children. It is about the children and people who lovingly and unselfishly made it a wonderful centre for healing. Their human stories told in this book will provide a record for all those associated with the hospital and those interested in the development of provision for hospitalised children as viewed through different peoples' eyes.

* * * * * *

Florence Nightingale's Prayer

'To hands that work and eyes that see,
Give wisdoms' heavenly lore,
That whole and sick and weak and strong,
May praise thee evermore.'

Contributed by Morag Orr (nee McGregor) former nursing student, Nightingale School of Nursing, Edinburgh Royal Infirmary. (1962-66). (The prayer is inscribed on a plaque in the nurses' dining room).

This book is dedicated to all sick people.

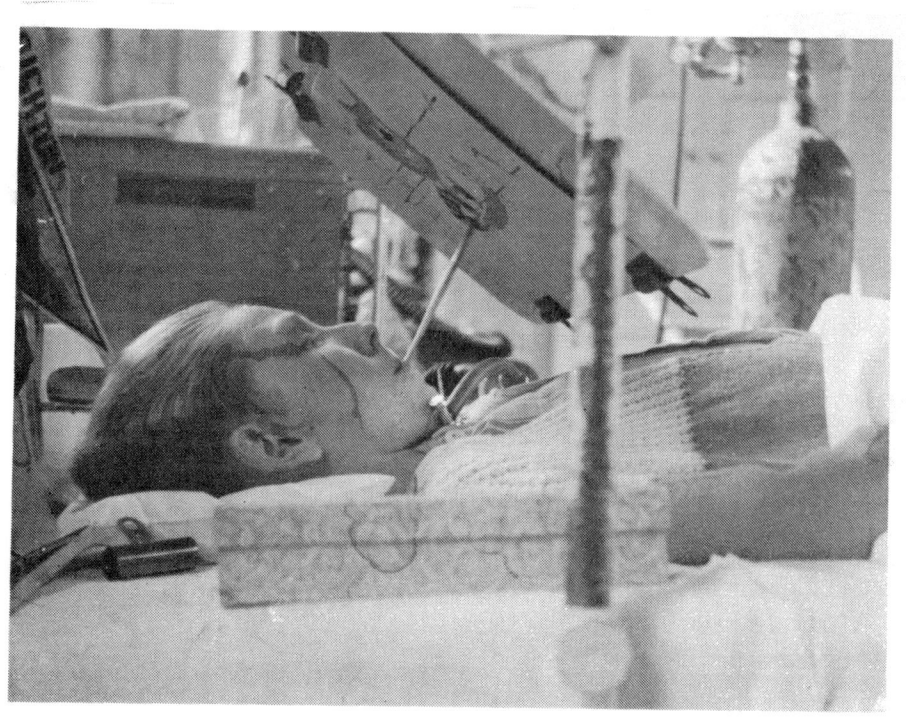

Painting by mouth

ACKNOWLEDGEMENTS

I would like to acknowledge the valuable assistance given to me by the following people in the making of this book.

Former patients for their stories and poems.
My wife Frances.
Mrs Marian Forbes for her typing advice and proof reading.
Dr. Nick Silva for his article on medical developments.
The late Joe Smith for giving so much time in the recounting of his memoirs.
Miss Muriel Taylor, former Head Teacher for supplying photographs and stories and writing her memoirs.
Mr Robert Wade, the hospital photographer and his staff for reproducing old photographs.
Miss Muriel Hayman, former Nursing Tutor, for supplying photographs and material.
The late Miss Marjorie Stratton, a former teacher who gave me her photographs and articles on Queen Mary's.
Dr. A.T. Piesowicz and members of the Child Health Management Team for granting permission to publish old photographs of staff and patients.
Parents and staff for so much encouragement and co-operation.
Sutton, Redhill and Merstham Public Libraries, East Surrey Hospital Library and Wellcome Foundation, whose staff answered many queries and supplied material.
Mr Gadfan Morris and his wife Margaret for proof reading and advice.
Mr Ross McClean and the TSB Bank Plc., Redhill, Surrey.
Mr Ron Hack for sending me the article on the Iron Age Camp.
Graham and Angela Green for advice and help with Marketing.
Mr. C. Blurton Director of Education, London Borough of Sutton, for granting permission to print extracts from the hospital school log books.
Mrs Valerie Turner for her advice.
The proprietors and staff of the corner stores, South Nutfield, for their Photocopying service.
Mr Barry Gandy NAS/UWT for advice.
Last but by no means least, my parents, sister Rita and her husband Jeff, brother Arthur and his wife Margaret.

The Hospital was opened in 1909 by John Burns, who was then President of the Local Government Board, as the "Children's Infirmary". Its purpose was to relieve the pressure on the accommodation for the sick poor of the Metropolis- " To bring them" as John Burns put it in his opening address, "out of the workhouses and on to the breezy downs of Surrey".

Radio Lollipop on the day of its offical opening.
10th December 1991

INTRODUCTION

There has been occupation of the Queen Mary's Hospital site since the Neolithic period (*New Stone Age).

The land on which Queen Mary's was built was purchased in 1896 by the Metropolitan Asylums Board for £13,550 from the Stanley Estates. When the buildings on the original 136 acre site were completed in 1906, it was called the Southern Hospital. It stood empty until 1909.

Originally designed as a convalescent fever hospital, but not needed for this purpose, it became available for other uses. It came about that when the Local Government Board proposed, as a means of relieving the pressure on the accommodation for the sick poor in the metropolis, that the Metropolitan Asylums Board should undertake the care of such sick children as were suitable for removal from the infirmaries, their request could at once be complied with.

The Board had already realised the advantage of treating sick London children in a country hospital. On 29th January 1909 the Hospital was opened by John Burns, President of the Local Government Board, with Dr. W.T. Gordon Pugh as Medical Superintendent. It became known as the 'Children's Infirmary'.

In 1914 Queen Mary became Patron of the Hospital. After her visit on the 14th May 1915 it was re-named Queen Mary's Hospital for Children in her honour.

Malnutrition, poor housing and sanitation were the causes of many diseases in the early part of the century. Fresh air and sunshine were recommended in the treatment of these illnesses.

In 1912, verandas, each containing 30 beds were added to 10 of the single storey ward blocks, enabling 300 children to lie in the open air, winter and summer, day and night, almost completely free from colds and infectious diseases. Considerable use was made of sunlight, and the courtyards opening only to the South, with the verandas on the three remaining sides, were ideal for the carrying out of this treatment. It became known as the sunshine hospital.

In the autumn of 1928 a further extension of the hospital began and the erection of a chapel, two single-storey ward blocks with verandas, and four nurses homes, together with a staff kitchen, services and rest-rooms was completed in 1930.

The London County Council was the Hospital authority, the Education authority, the Tuberculosis authority and the Poor Law authority of the County, the majority of patients came from one or other of these services. A substantial number of patients were received from the voluntary hospitals of London. Parents were assessed according to their means.

In 1937 Sister Elizabeth Kenny from Australia was given every facility to demonstrate her methods for the treatment of polio at Queen Mary's and it became internationally famous as a treatment centre for this unorthodox but very successful method.

In 1943 a physiotherapist, Mrs Eirene Collis, began work in the Cerebral Palsy Unit. Her treatment eventually gained international repute and people came from all over the world to study her methods.

The fifties brought more changes to the hospital. With the advances in medicine made during the war years there was a decline in the number of patients; and diseases, such as polio, were virtually wiped out. At the same time the Fountain Hospital in Tooting, where the First World War heroine Edith Cavell trained as a nurse, was looking for new accommodation. The Fountain Hospital catered for children with Special Needs, and had its own hospital school.

In 1959 as a consequence of the Mental Health Act the children from the Fountain Hospital were transferred to Queen Mary's. It became the first comprehensive children's hospital in the United Kingdom.

More additions were made to the hospital over the years. These included an enclosed swimming pool for therapeutic and recreational purposes; an architect designed Pets Corner and a block of four flatlets enabled children who could not go home to enjoy family life with their parents or to be used when the parents needed to learn how to use special equipment. The Drapers school enabling children to be taught in a purpose built environment, as well as a sports pavilion with a heated open air swimming pool for the use of staff, and the Friends Centre i.e. a canteen and social centre run by the League of Friends. It had its own chapel, a resident Anglican Chaplain and a miniature railway.

In 1979 the first hospital radio for children started at Queen Mary's. On the 10th December 1991 the Radio Lollipop Centre was opened by John Leslie of the BBC Blue Peter programme. He arrived by helicopter, landing on the football pitch.

With advances in medicine and a consequent reduction in admissions plus a shorter length of stay for those admitted, Queen Mary's shrank in size. Eventually it was closed at the former site in Carshalton on the 30th November 1993.

I am very proud to have been a teacher at Queen Mary's.

*Ref: AWG Lowther FSA
'Report on excavations at the Site of the Early Iron Age Camp in the Grounds of Queen Mary's Hospital, Carshalton, Surrey'.

John Leslie arriving by Helicopter on the football pitch to open the new Radio Lollipop centre on the 10th December 1991

Ernie winning the Surrey Cross Country championship at Chessington Surrey, from the English International Mike Maynard (135) January 1960

ABOUT THE AUTHOR

I was born in Bermondsey, in London, in 1937. During the War, I moved with my parents and brother, to Tooting and attended the local Infants and Junior Schools, before going on to the Bec Grammar School.

My main interests at school were sport, especially running, and history. Before leaving school I joined the Hercules Athletic Club and continued my athletics career with them. I had joined the Boys' Brigade at the age of 12 and was awarded the Queen's Badge in 1954.

On leaving school I did two years training as a telephone engineer. After qualifying in 1956, I was called up for National Service in the RAF. During this time I represented the RAF at middle distance running.

Returning to civilian life in 1958 I went back to my job as a telephone engineer. In September 1960 I started a new career as a student teacher at the College of St. Mark and St. John, Chelsea.

Prior to entering college I represented Great Britain at middle distance running and though tipped by one of the national newspapers for a 5000 metre place in the Olympic team 1960, my career came to a premature end before this, due to recurring Achilles tendon breakdown.

Ernie(left) seen here with Frank Sando(centre) and Alan Perkins after winning the Rochester 5 mile road race in record time (24min.45seconds.) November 1959. Frank is a former Olympic 10,000 metre runner, international cross country champion and England team captain. Alan is a former England National cross country champion.

Dr. Silva and Nurse Helen Cox taken after Dr. Silva's talk on The History of Queen Mary's

CHAPTER 1

Queen Mary's Hospital for Children

by Dr. Nicholas C. Silva

I studied medicine at St George's Hospital, Tooting, London.

My first exposure to paediatrics was as a student in 1984 at Queen Mary's Hospital. The hospital had not received students for some time and so it was a new experience for both them and us and I was in the first group to visit the vast expanse of the hospital. We were met with enthusiastic staff from all fields. The medical staff were keen to teach and the nursing staff were also very welcoming and full of useful information. Most importantly, the parents of the children and the children themselves were happy to recount their illnesses - yet again and put up with further prodding of tummies. I left the attachment having learnt not just about illness but also about children. Having been the most enjoyable part of my training, it was a small step to decide on Paediatrics as a career. I was later to return to the hospital as a member of staff and have worked at both old and new sites.

My interest in the history of the hospital started when I was looking up references in the library. I accidentally came across some annual reports from the 1960's and realised that there were other sources of information scattered around. It has been a fascinating exercise looking at the old nursing records and registers and I am pleased to have been asked to contribute to this history.

QUEENS MARY'S HOSPITAL FOR CHILDREN, CARSHALTON

Dr. Nicholas C. Silva

When Queen Mary's Hospital For Children opened its doors to the young population of London and the surrounding area in 1909, medicine was very different from that which we are used to now, some 85 years later. The Infirmary was to open around the start of a century that was to push medical knowledge forward tremendously.

It would not only be the development of new treatment that was to change the health of the child; social changes were also vitally important in controlling disease and improving nutrition.

Before looking at the way in which Queen Mary's Hospital cared for children and helped in the development of paediatric care it is appropriate to review the provision of health care for children.

In the middle of the 19th century there had been opposition to the development of children's hospitals. At that time it was clear that responsibility for the care of the child, whether well or sick, was that of one person - the mother. In 1843 there were more than 2000 patients in the hospitals of London; of the 2000 less than 30 were under 10 years of age. At that time 21000 children under the age of 10 died annually, in London.

Children received their medical care through dispensaries; one of which was to develop into Great Ormond Street in London, founded in 1852. Often the family doctor was the only person available to care for the child at home. There was no access to the high technology that now saves so many lives.

Nowadays, we are used to the concept of a doctor who only looks after children. However, the first paediatrician had been George Frederick Still at the end of the 19th century. Three years before the opening of Queen Mary's Hospital he was to become the first Professor of Paediatrics.

Towards the end of the century society was accepting the notion of children's hospitals and centres of various sizes and in differing locations were to develop.

Let us look a little closer at the situation around the time of the opening of Queen Mary's Hospital. The general health of the population in the early part of the century was poor and the military turned down many potential recruits for the first World War on grounds of poor nutrition. In 1906 over 11 children per thousand born, died on their first day of life. About 38 per thousand died before they were one year old. Almost one in 10 children did not reach their tenth birthday. Premature births and serious abnormalities were responsible for most of the early deaths. Infectious diseases also took their toll. In the early years of life whooping cough, measles, diphtheria, tuberculosis, pneumonia and diarrhoea are just a few of the illnesses that claimed thousands of lives each year.

A couple of years previous to the opening of Queen Mary's Hospital in 1909, the School Health Service was developed. The School Doctor examined all children in school, at no cost to the parents. Many were found to need treatment although this did not legally have to be provided. One of the main aims was the provision of appropriate nutrition for the school aged child and this was one of the responsibilities of the School Doctor. This was often the only contact the child had with a doctor. There still remained a gap in provision for the pre-school aged child. The introduction of Health visitors did not come into force until some years later. Young children could go long periods of time without medical supervision, and illness was often not easily recognised. By the time illness was identified it may have had serious and permanent effects.

The medical profession had limited investigations and treatment. Blood tests were basic and very time consuming, the discovery of X rays was in 1895 and there were no antibiotics. Koch was responsible for the identification of the organism that causes tuberculosis in 1882 and insulin was not identified until 1922. Queen Mary's Hospital was therefore to play an important part in developing paediatric care. It soon built up a world wide reputation, resulting in many doctors visiting from abroad to learn and take back innovative treatment to their own countries.

With this background of prevailing illness available, intervention staff to care for the children were appointed to work at the new Children's Infirmary.

Dr. Pugh, was the Medical Superintendent. He had initially looked after mostly adults and had a background of being a surgeon. He earned the sum of £700 in the first year although he also had a free house together with heating and electricity, free laundry and a gardener. By 1934 he was on the princely sum of £1500 per annum. Dr. Pugh remained in post until his retirement in 1937.

Other hospitals in London looked after many children who were transferred to the country for long term care and The Infirmary took over the care of many of these patients. Some of these children would have been in wards with adults and probably had few children of their own age in hospital with them. Queen Mary's accepted children from all over the London area. The admissions book indicates that children came from Paddington, Hackney, Mile End, Bethnal Green, Poplar and other areas.

Being in such a country location had a number of advantages. In an era when fresh air was seen as an elixir, the most was made of the Surrey countryside.

In the Manchester Guardian of July 26th 1924 an article spoke of using light for treatment which was being pioneered in this country at Queen Mary's Hospital. Dr. Rollier of Switzerland had invented this therapy.

The title was 'Fear no more the heat of the sun' and the article talked of a 'sunlight cure in England'. The report contains descriptions of some children having their legs covered in white lotion to prevent burning whilst others were 'burnt to the colour of Zeus'. The percentage of cures in cases of hip and spinal disease were said to be 'very high' if caught early and it is noted that there was not a 'dark or stuffy corner to the whole place'.

The paper described a little boy with paralysis to part of his face. He used a mirror in which he produced grimaces to make the sides of his face appear the same; he had been told that once he could whistle properly he could return to his mother.

The article goes on to talk of the 'Magnetic advantages from whirlpools'.

Unfortunately, as we are well aware, sunlight is far from inevitable but a dull day was well provided for. In some of the ward blocks there was light producing equipment. Children were exposed to this clothed in very little and had small protective glasses reminiscent of swimming goggles. By contrast the nursing staff wore outfits that must have been impermeable to the beneficial properties of the treatment, covered from head to toe with their uniforms and wearing what looked like welding masks.

Dr. Pugh in 1927 wrote about the early treatment of tuberculosis hip disease.

"This is the time time to apply intensive constitutional treatment - continuous life in the open air, heliotherapy, good food, cod-liver oil - combined with effective traction".

Dr. Pugh appeared to be a great believer in the saying "prevention is better than cure". Primarily he was an orthopaedic surgeon and he was particularly concerned with the prevention of deformity secondary to tuberculosis of bones and joints and that related to polio. He strove to avoid the wasting of muscles that occurs when we do not use them. Anyone who has had their limb in a plaster cast will know that little time is required for this to happen. Many of the children were immobilised not for a few weeks, as is the case with a broken bone, but for many months or even years.

He worked on the design of frames and carriages to accommodate children requiring orthopaedic intervention. These allowed them to be mobile whilst traction was applied, the fastenings appeared to be out of the way of wandering little hands looking for freedom and there was even an arrangement for the use of a bed pan without disturbing the position of the back.

To produce the equipment through the years has needed a dedicated team. The engineering workshop was essential and a department still exists which is able to adapt items for individual usage as well as producing work from scratch.

It seems that the children took exercise in liberal amounts, whatever their abilities and restrictions imposed on them by their therapy. This meant that some children exercised in the open air if they could only move their arms and legs. Photographs show large numbers of children in the yards at the back of the ward blocks exercising under the direction of a nurse or physiotherapist.

Some children spent long periods of time immobilised. They were at risk of developing pressure sores as the parts of the skin that were in contact with the hard surfaces could have broken down. However this seems to be hardly mentioned in the writings of the hospital and seems to have occurred infrequently. Care of any wounds was intensive; Dr. Pugh expected nurses to change the dressings 4 hourly which could mean that a nurse could change 100 dressings in a day.

Wherever there is a large number of people in close proximity there is always the risk of contagious diseases spreading. Being in a hospital need not mean that this is less likely to happen, even if the wards are separated from each other, as was the case in the design of Queen Mary's Hospital. The original purpose of the hospital was as a hospital for adults with infectious disease and so the wards are positioned over the many acres. One infectious disease that caused a problem in the early years was ringworm and with the initiation of Wood's Light, which gives out a light of a certain wavelength in the ultraviolet region, it was possible to examine all of the children in the hospital. The examiner shone the light over the children's skin and looked for the tell tale green patches. Dr. Pugh had something to say on the matter.

"The procedure is a rapid one, for the ambulant boys are dealt with at the rate of about 60 an hour, the girls and recumbent cases naturally taking longer".

Wherever there is illness it is accompanied by death. Death registers are available and these may be examined to see the early patterns of mortality.

As stated earlier, most of the children looked after at Queen Mary's Hospital in the early years were not acutely ill, with conditions that were immediately threatening their lives. Even so deaths were commonplace.

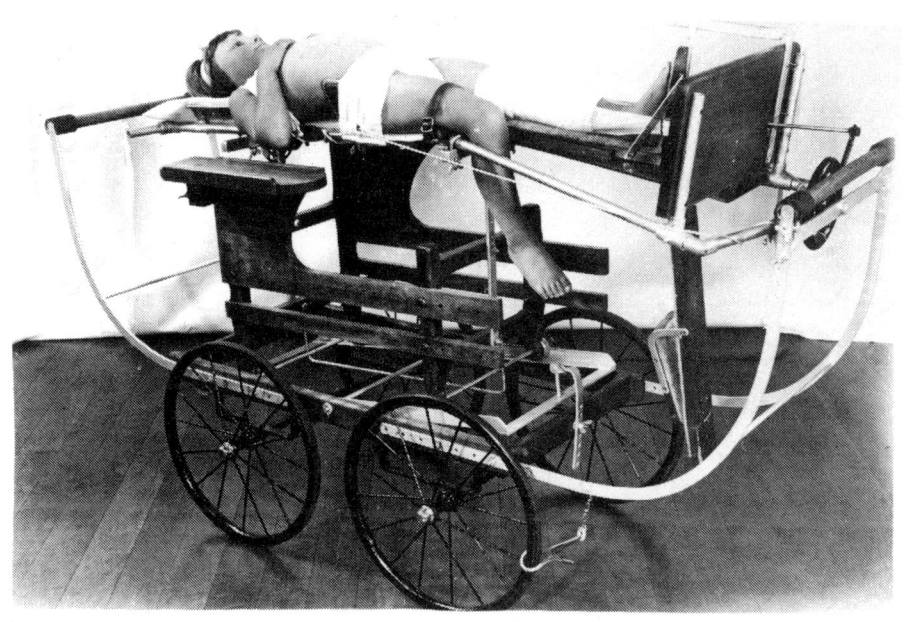

A carriage made by medical engineering

Around 80 children died annually in the first years of the hospital. At the time of the highest number of deaths, at the beginning of the Second World War, 3 children were taken to the mortuary per week.

Analysis of the first register reveals some of the epidemiology of the time. The recording of the cause of death was usually a single diagnosis. Each entry seems to have been written by the same hand - possibly Dr. Pugh's and there are notably few mistakes.

Occasionally others notes were added, such as the result of a post mortem. These were carried out in few cases and the vast percentage occurred in children who had died from tuberculosis, perhaps reflecting Dr. Pugh's main interest. Incidentally, the register also records staff deaths there being 38 beds available for staff in the 1930's.

Most deaths were in children less than one year old.

Just as infection was important nationally it played a large part in the causation of death of people in hospital. At the time treatment was minimal and immunisation almost non existent. In 1940 the diphtheria immunisation was introduced, and in 1953 the BCG against tuberculosis. Queen Mary's Hospital was one of the first hospitals in the country to be involved with research trials using the measles vaccine which followed in the 1960's.

The four commonest causes of death in 1910 were:-
Tuberculosis   15 cases
Marasmus   15 cases
Pneumonia   14 cases
Whooping Cough   7 cases

Marasmus is still familiar to us now, but not in this country. Marasmic children are those who are not putting on weight and who may die of starvation and the consequences of an inadequate diet. They have poor growth, wasting of their muscles and the child's kidneys and heart may fail to work correctly. That which is familiar to us now on television from other parts of the world (pictures of the famines of Africa) was familiar in London before the Second World War.

In 1931 Queen Mary's Hospital became the official receiver for children with marasmus for the London County Council.

Other causes of death were polio, heart disease due to rheumatic fever, meningitis and convulsions.

There was no treatment for tuberculosis at this time. Deaths occurred secondary to lung, kidney, bone involvement and meningitis.

It may have been that not all of the diagnoses in the registers were correct, with our knowledge now we may have identified a different cause. The child dying at a few days or weeks of age may have had a metabolic disorder at that time unidentified.

Some marasmic children also died due to secondary infection; pneumonia or measles for example.

Most children who have been in hospital now are in for a few days only. Many operations are carried out on the day of admission and the child goes home in the afternoon. In the past this was very different.

From 1926 to 1927 the average length of stay for a diabetic was 97 days, for scurvy (a lack of vitamin C) 172 days and for rickets (soft bones) 235 days and this was for those children who were discharged. Even bearing in mind that this was predominantly a convalescent hospital some of the lengths of stay are remarkable. For many children this was not a hospital but a home, and a home for a significant length of time.

Some children saw year after year in their beds or in their carriages. Between the years 1948 and 1958 the average length of stay fell from over 100 to 30 days.

Keeping the children occupied for such times must have been difficult. There were scouts and guide groups and also, seemingly, a number of fetes in the grounds and possibly coronation and jubilee parties also.

Through the 1920s the hospital continued to develop. In 1926, 60 beds for rheumatic fever were opened. Rheumatic fever is now unusual in this country. It develops after an infection that may lead to destruction of heart valves or involvement of the brain. As well as dealing with rheumatic fever and its complications, the unit was also heavily involved with research especially bacteriological. This unit also rapidly grew reaching 390 beds in 1938. As social conditions improved rheumatic fever decreased.

An outdoor, but heated pool was built in 1927 leading to world wide coverage. For this country, it was an innovation and added further to the exercise that children undertook to develop weakened muscles.

As well as the medical staff the hospital had many other therapists and nursing staff all essential to paediatric care.

Physiotherapy continues to be an important part of paediatric care. When tuberculosis and polio were rife there must have been a tremendous workload.

As well as physiotherapists, staff for massage were employed. The massage department reached 15 staff in the 30's. The departmental sister earned £100 per year increasing in increments of £5 to £125. If recommended at the end of 8 years service this was increased to £135 per year. This was seen as a generous salary. When the hospital had to advertise at a lower rate the job remained unfilled.

The respected name of Queen Mary's Hospital spread widely and many health workers came from all parts of the world to visit, learn and share their knowledge.

In 1937 one of the many overseas visitors arrived. Elizabeth Kenny was a 6 foot, Australian, wounded nurse, limping between the beds within one hour of arriving.

The Daily Express wrote, "So secret is the visit that not even the nurses working in the same wing of the buildings in which she works know of her mission. To them she is just a visiting nurse gaining experience".

Elizabeth Kenny was a pioneer in the treatment of infantile paralysis and diplegia (a form of cerebral palsy affecting mostly the legs). Her methods of treatment, including brine baths, were viewed as radical but seemed a natural extension of what Queen Mary's Hospital was already doing.

Elizabeth Kenny's treatment was based on 5 principles.
1. Maintenance of a bright mental outlook.
2. Maintenance of impulse (i.e. nerve impulse).
3. Hydrotherapy and remedial exercises.
4. Maintenance of circulation.
5. Avoidance of generally accepted methods of immobilisation.

Outdoor heated pool.

She was once offered £20,000 for her secret but turned it down saying that it would be wrong to profit from her discovery. General treatment was of a good diet, suitable surroundings, fresh air. Staff also paid attention to cleanliness and 'regulation of the bowels'.

The papers reported a daily improvement in cases, which the hospital staff had earlier declared to be hopeless. Her stay, initially set for a few weeks, was extended to one year and her experience was handed on to others who continued to work at Queen Mary's Hospital.

Medicine continued to develop over the years. With the bombings suffered during World War II the hospital was evacuated. However, even during this time the hospital continued to implement new ideas.

Queen Mary's Hospital opened the Cerebral Palsy Unit in 1943. This engaged in the total assessment of children suspected of, or having Cerebral Palsy. There was an inpatient unit and a parental advice clinic. The clinic had to be extended to North London because of the distances from where some families were referred. From 1954 to 1956, 206 children were referred. Cerebral Palsy was one of the areas of research in the hospital.

Throughout the history of the hospital there has been opportunity for research, and staff have carried out much original and important work. Bacteriological studies, including investigating Rheumatic Fever, as mentioned earlier, and work with the introduction of antibiotics, treatment of polio, investigation into metabolic disorders, cystic fibrosis, moderate and severe learning difficulties, Downs Syndrome and Spina Bifida are just a few of the subjects visited at various times.

Once the Second World War ended, because of war damage, there were 840 beds rather than the 1200 or so.

In 1948 the hospital came under the auspices of the NHS. This involved covering a larger area, which had a greater population than in the past and it was also the time of much advancement in medicine. The illnesses that had been so prevalent in the initial years gradually waned.

The work of QMH changed to accommodate these advances. It became increasingly a general children's hospital and in the mid

Outdoor exercises

1950's, under the eye of Dr. David Lawson, the Outpatient's Department, an isolation unit and redevelopment of the pathology services were among the projects that were implemented. More children who were acutely ill were admitted and the long stay patients became less common.

During the late 1950's there was talk of major changes for the hospital. Because of decreasing admissions and shorter stays in hospital beds the Government proposed that the children could be looked after in other hospitals more local to where they lived. Meanwhile in Tooting, the Fountain Hospital wanted larger premises. The Fountain cared for people with learning difficulties and was where St George's Hospital is now. Therefore it was felt that Queen Mary's Hospital could close its doors. The battle over the hospital was long but the protests were partly listened to and so it was that the Fountain and Queen Mary's amalgamated to fit in with one proposal inherent to the 1959 Mental Health Act, that of bringing together mental and physical health. The beds were split between the specialities. QMH had become the first comprehensive children's hospital in the country.

The philosophy for visiting children in hospital is now to allow children to have ready access to parents, siblings and relatives. Many parents manage to stay with their children during their hospitalisation and visiting for parents, and to a lesser extent other relatives and friends, is often 'open' so that they may visit at any time. On the other hand visiting was strict in the 1960's. In 1964 visiting for people other than parents was on Wednesdays and Fridays from 5 to 5.30 p.m. and Sunday 2 to 4 p.m. Otherwise the ward sister gave permission for guests to visit at other times. Siblings under the age of 15 were not generally allowed to visit unless their sib had been a patient for a long period of time; defined as more than 6 months. If it was not possible to leave children at home then their parents left them in the playroom situated at the front gate. An orderly staffed this on Sundays otherwise an adult had to stay with them.

The layout of the wards meant that each could contain a group of similar cases, this makes it easier for medical and nursing staff. In addition age groups were also accommodated in different wards. In the 1960's this was the composition of the hospital:-

Acute surgical, eye and dental	20 beds
Acute surgical and orthopaedic	40
Acute surgery	20
Long stay medical (girls)	20
Long stay medical (boys)	40
Acute medical	60
Acute medical (infants)	20
Acute medical and ENT	40
Acute medical (isolation)	30
Poliomyelitis	20
Children's psychiatry	20
Orthopaedic	60
Long stay surgical	20
Muscular dystrophy	30
Cerebral Palsy Unit	20
Learning Difficulties	320

In the past, the size of the hospital has put it into the record books - the Guinness Book of Records has listed Queen Mary's Hospital as the largest children's hospital in the UK.

Throughout the last 20 years there have been further changes. Modern medicine means many other departments are now involved. We rely heavily on adequate laboratory services, radiology departments for X rays, ultrasound and production of other images of the body, pharmacies to supply an increasing list of drugs and increasing technology can be seen both attached to patients and being used in investigation and treatment. The list goes on.

The Cerebral Palsy Unit was to close in the early 70s. The polio unit was to close shortly afterwards having had more than 2000 children through its doors.

A quite large dental department developed, not just accepting children from outside the hospital but looking after the dental health of the longer stay children.

Children with disabilities had always been a large part of the work at Queen Mary's Hospital. More and more children were quite rightly becoming able to live out of hospital and it was realised that a centre to assess these children was needed.

In 1982 with the hard work of Dr. Josephine Hammond, including fund raising, the Rainbow Centre was opened, specifically to assess handicapped children. As developments in treating childhood cancer progressed it was useful to develop a link with the Royal Marsden Hospital: this occurred with the appointment of Dr. Simon Meller. Many other medical staff have been essential in developing services for children attending the hospital.

In 1984 Tadworth Court separated from Great Ormond Street. Many of the children who were at Tadworth had orthopaedic conditions or orthopaedic complications of their illnesses. Queen Mary's Hospital continued its tradition for orthopaedic care by taking over the orthopaedic care of the children at Tadworth.

Over the last decade bed numbers have dwindled further and planning for the future has been ongoing. Gradually the prognosis has become clear.

Paediatrics has changed over the century. Progress in both medical and social areas had largely conquered the illnesses of the initial days. Now paediatric respiratory disease, cardiology (heart), endocrinology (hormones), paediatric surgery, immunology (the body's defences against disease), neurology (the nervous system), psychiatry and neonatology (care of the newborn baby) are some of the specially developed services represented at Queen Mary's Hospital and St. Helier's. The leading causes of death in children are now prematurity, sudden infant death (cot death), accidents, and cancer. Now the chances of not surviving the early days of life is about 5 per thousand babies born and there are only 11 deaths per thousand children up to the age of 5 years. Comparing these figures with those noted at the beginning of this chapter, we can easily see the improvement in the outcome of childhood.

Hospital provision too has developed. There are no longer the large numbers of children within institutions. The facilities that we now require to investigate and treat children have changed. Many children are admitted for a short period of time and more and more children are cared for in the community nursing team.

Childrens' hospitals throughout the country have closed or remain under threat. Builders have recently turned the Belgrave Hospital in Kennington into "Luxury Flats". They have retained the original brickwork that will inform future generations of the original purpose of the building. Passers-by can still see The Royal Waterloo Hospital for Women and Children in a state of disrepair in London. Questions have even been posed over the future of some of the largest children's hospitals in the Country.

Now that Queen Mary's Hospital has been relocated it has enabled most of the services needed for the care of the child to be easily available on the one site. What ever the future of paediatric medicine and the outlook for Queen Mary's Hospital, the Infirmary and Queen Mary's Hospital, Carshalton can be proud of its contribution towards the care of the child.

Natalie Phillips Learning about Christopher Columbus.

Sadly Natalie died on the 9th August 1995, a year after writing this story for my book. A bright and courageous child who radiated happiness wherever she went. Natalie made light of her problems and was always smiling and laughing. She will be greatly missed by all who knew her.

CHAPTER 2

PATIENT'S SECTION

BEWARE, JOSIE, BEWARE
By Natalie Phillips
(one of my former pupils)

Once there lived a little girl called Tina. She had a horse called Josie, who was four years old. They lived in a cottage near the wood. Tina's father was a wealthy person, so he drove around in a white and gold Rolls Royce. One day Tina was out riding her horse Josie out in the meadow, suddenly there came a voice from behind the bushes. "What are you doing in my meadow?"

"I'm riding my horse in this meadow, that's what". All of a sudden a pack of hunters came walking by, they saw Josie and one of them said, "Get that horse quick, before she gets away." Luckily Josie managed to get away and cantered back home in to her stables. One night when everything was quiet, Tina crept out of bed and went out into the stables to feed Josie then went back to her bed and when she was asleep, Josie put her head in the window and got a couple of carrots (large) in the kitchen. Then later that evening something extremely terrifying happened; a man with a mask on came into the stables and captured Josie from her home in Yorkshire. The news was spread everywhere, cameramen came to take pictures for the local paper and it was in the T.V. News. Crowds of people came to see this extraordinary sight. Later that day Tina felt so upset, she cried whilst in church when she got home she reported it to the police and the kidnapper was found and put in jail for 17 years. The man was 25. But he wouldn't last long because doctors said he had a serious illness and would only live for about 10 years. Years had passed and everyone was happy once again because the kidnapper had committed suicide and Tina got a new horse called Snowy. But Tina's brother Steve had ran away from home and luckily was found but he was ill. He recovered so quickly though. Everyone was happy yet again.

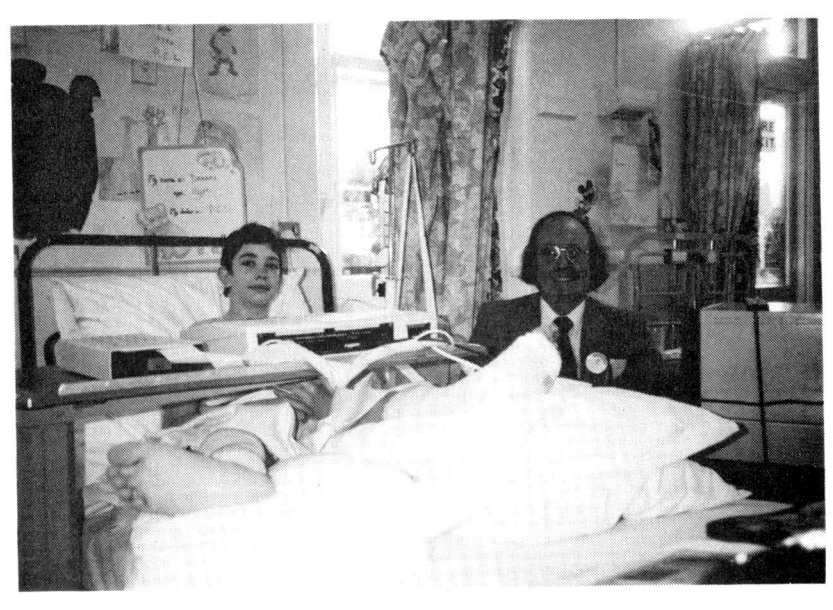

Daniel and Ernie
A lesson on the computer.

DANIEL'S STORY

My name is Daniel and I am 12 years old. I have been coming to Queen Mary's Hospital for Children since I was a baby. Soon after I was born I had neonatal Meningitis. I had fits with the Meningitis and the side effects of this left me with Hydrocephalus and Hemiplegia (Hydrocephalus is also known as water on the brain). I had my first shunt put in when I was six weeks old and have had three more since then. Hemiplegia is paralysis down one side of the body - in my case it affects the left side of my body, but luckily for me it is a very mild paralysis.

I have had quite a few in-patient days at Queen Mary's and over the years my family and I have seen many changes. The hospital was very busy and had lots of patients who came from all different parts of the country, but as time went on the hospital had fewer and fewer patients.

The hospital had a lovely Pets Corner that I used to go to quite often. It had lots of different animals such as goats, rabbits, guinea pigs, chinchilla and different breeds of birds such as budgies and cockatiels.

The hospital also had a Radio Lollipop Centre which was great fun to go to as there were lots of different activities to do and you could also see where the records were played from. In the evenings and at the weekends the people who worked at Radio Lollipop would come to the wards to chat and spend time with the children. We would have competitions and there were always prizes for the winners. They would also ask us what records we wanted played and it was great to hear something you had asked for being played on the radio. The people who worked at the Radio Lollipop Centre were very kind as they didn't get paid for spending time with the children.

We also had to have school lessons when we were in hospital so we didn't get out of going to school. This is where I met Mr Earl. He has been my teacher since I was five years old; whenever I have been in Queen Mary's. The thing I liked best about school lessons was the computer. Mr Earl was very kind and would let me use it quite a lot if it wasn't being used by other children.

I was very sad when Queen Mary's, Carshalton closed and moved to the new site at St. Helier's Hospital. It was such a nice hospital to be in and has been a big part of my life.

Esme receiving her award.

"STAR AWARD FOR BRAVE ESME"

"From the Beccles and Bungay Journal, June 14, 1991". with kind permission of Eastern Counties Newspapers Ltd.

The courage of a nine-year-old Halesworth Brownie has won her an award for bravery.

Pain, a wheelchair, crutches and numerous hospital visits have been familiar facts of life for Esme Trussler, of Bramfield, as she has battled to overcome the handicap of having one leg shorter than the other.

But on Sunday the courage with which Esme has grappled with the problem was recognised when Suffolk Guides' County Commissioner Janet Courtice presented her with the Guide movement's national Star of Merit bravery award.

Esme had already won the admiration of her family - mother Lynne, father Chris and two older brothers, Mark and Dean - long before Sunday's presentation was made at Halesworth United Reformed Church.

Mrs Trussler explained: "Esme was born with one leg shorter than the other and last July she was taken to Carshalton Hospital in Surrey.

"She had a fixator attached to her leg, a big metal contraption with four pins screwed into the bone.

"Each day she had to turn a key to get a millimetre of growth".

The stretching process continued until October during which time the bone grew by two-and a-half inches.

The fixator, which had to remain in place until the new bone was formed, was removed about two months ago, and Esme had to go to Great Ormond Street, London, to have the plaster cast removed.

Now Esme, who had to use a wheelchair while the treatment was in progress, has been able to get around since Christmas with the help of crutches.

"I wouldn't like to have gone through what she has gone through," said Mrs Trussler. "It was very painful at times towards the end of the treatment but she didn't complain.

"There were lots of sleepless nights, and disruption to the family, but she has been brilliant.

"The leg is still not long enough, and we are going back to Great Ormond Street in November to see how she is getting on."

Despite the crutches, and the pain, Esme is a regular attender at school and enjoys her time with the 2nd Halesworth Brownies where she has impressed her Brownie friends and Brown Owl Alison Nichols with her cheerful courage.

Esme's story

The day I went into Queen Mary's was a really hot day.
We had a long way to come from home.
We went to find the ward I was being admitted to, it was called Mrs Tiggy Winkle ward. My ward was a long ward with lots of boys and girls in it.
My mum stayed at the hospital with me, she slept in a building called Hamilton House.
We had duvets on our beds.
All the nurses were very nice.
The day after I went in I had to have an X-ray and a blood test, I remember going to the toy library and the lady saw my plaster on my arm where I had my blood test, she said I was very brave and gave me a bar of chocolate. At Queen Mary's there was also a pets corner, which Mum and me had a look around.
The day after that I had my operation. The day I had the operation I was taken to the building where the operating theatre was, we had to go in electric lorries, Mum came with me and a nurse. I had magic cream on my hand. I don't remember much more about the operation until much later in the day, when my leg and ankle was hurting. There was a boy in the next bed to mine who was in traction and wouldn't keep still.
My Gran and Grandad and Auntie came for the day following my operation. I had lots of cards and some presents, one was a keeper, that is a small animal whose back opens up and you can store things in it and then lock it up. I had lots of nose bleeds while I was in hospital. I remember one nurse I didn't like she held an ice pack on my nose and it hurt because it was so cold. There was different nurses at night, one was a man. One evening the ice-cream man came round and stopped outside of my ward, after he had finished his rounds and what ice-cream he had left he brought to my ward. While I was in my ward it was very hot and the nurses made the children ice lollies with medicine pots and tongue depressors for lolly sticks. One nurse spilt someone's bottle of Ribena and people at first thought it was blood when they saw it on the floor. Most of the wards at

Queen Mary's were in different blocks, it was a very old hospital but I liked it there very much. I was in for a week. I remember saying goodbye to the nurses when I left. As it was school summer holidays, we all had TV's on our bed side lockers. I had long hair down to my bottom and because I was laying down a lot it used to get in a tangle. One day a nurse plaited it for me in a basked weave. While I was there the Queen Mother had her 90th birthday and some of the wards had a party out on the grass; a nurse got me a wheelchair so I could go and join in, - the wheel had a flat tyre. We were given sweets, stickers, and a frisbee and other things, I didn't really want to go at first but I enjoyed it. We had pin boards over our bed heads so we could stick things on it. After our operations we were given a certificate for being brave. There were trees around the hospital and I remember seeing a squirrel when I left. Mum said she saw a fox there in the grounds one morning. Mum had her meals in the staff canteen.

About nine months after I had to go in to Queen Mary's again to have my fixator removed, this time it was in a school term and there was teachers on the ward I remember Mr Ernie Earl. He gave me things to do and didn't make me do things I didn't want or feel like doing. I wasn't in hospital more than a few days this time, I'd had my hair cut short by now. I remember the nurses waving goodbye to me.

My Queen Mary's Story : By Shajida Khanam

Being in a new country was strange enough, but when it meant that you were going to be admitted to hospital straight away, this was even more frightening for a nine year old. My entire life was turned upside down when, one morning I found to my horror that I could no longer walk or make any physical movement. Being without family or friends in an all new environment, with people around me speaking a language which I did not speak or understand, left me drained of all the little energy I had.

The first few days of what was to be a very long stay at hospital was a chapter of my life in which I experienced a great deal of anguish -even though everyone around me tried their best to make light of the situation. Today, I can still conjure up the memories and images that were around me, along with my deepest fears. Whatever I do in order to forget the unhappiness I endured, the memories stored inside, hinders me from trying to forget the past. I guess the whole process of trying to fully understand what happened to me and to overcome my anxieties will take time but, in time, I hope I will have the strength to close that sad chapter of my life, which sometimes now seems as though it was a bad nightmare.

The medical term for my condition was the rare Guillain Barré Syndrome and the only medication was continuous Physiotherapy. It was then decided that my home for the next few weeks was going to be what was then Ward B2. B2 was a children's ward with a friendly and happy atmosphere; however, not being able to communicate in English caused a number of problems, but due to everyone adopting a friendly approach, my sadness and anxieties were set at ease. To overcome the language barrier the playworker for B2 devised a picture card containing all the important aspects of life, such as eating, sleeping, going to the toilet and so on. The whole situation now sounds like a farce, but back then for me it was survival. It was as if I was a toddler learning to speak from the beginning and was being told the fundamental aspects of speech. I have to admit it was very hard for everyone involved, I recall how annoyed I used to get when people took ages understanding what I was trying to say. However, with the help and constant support of everyone, I managed to overcome these problems.

There were various activities aimed at keeping children amused and occupied, however nothing prevented me from missing my family who visited me frequently but not as often as I would have liked. I remember a particular one I enjoyed very much, it was called 'Frustration'. That I guess explains exactly how I felt.

One can say that I learnt the English language during my stay at hospital. The few people whom I have told about my illness find it extremely hard to believe that once I could not speak English, walk, or do all the many things I now take for granted. For instance, for the first few months I could not even grip a pen; now for University I have to write individual essays of up to three to four thousand words. My Mum's nightmare is finally over and when friends and relatives ask her about me she describes my life as being a 'miracle'. I guess you cannot argue with that. My Mum was my foundation and always used to say to me that, "One day you will walk and do all the things that you used to do". Which for reasons she could not explain suddenly got taken away from me.

I was at B2 for a long time, and soon I became familiar with everyone and everything. It was as though I found myself a new family. It was here I celebrated my Tenth Birthday with the whole Ward. The nurses were very kind and provided a beautiful birthday cake. Emotionally, I settled down. As the days passed I fell into a routine. The happiest day of my life was when I re-took my first step. The joy I felt was indescribable. For me it was as though I was given a new life and another chance. This glimmer of hope gave me such a boost that I began to concentrate and work harder during the Physiotherapy sessions. The progress I made following my long road to making a full recovery was gradual, until I was able to walk with the aid of a leg brace. Soon after I was discharged, a joyous occasion but a sad one too, as it meant saying goodbye to all the many people who had contributed to my recovery and helped me emotionally.

I know I am a very lucky person and have a great deal to be thankful for. I have come far but have yet to reach my ambition in life. I will be eternally grateful to all those wonderful people at Queen Mary's Hospital who made my long stay such a carefree and enjoyable time. I know it is hard to believe hospitals as being fun places, but truly, for me it really was.

I would like to take this opportunity to thank all those who looked after me so well during my stay at B2. I would also like to thank my family for all their encouragement and faith in me.

The End.

WE NEVER HAD IT SO GOOD

by Stuart Oliver

It was with a great sense of pride that I was asked to write this chapter on Queen Mary's Hospital which covers the late 1950s to mid-'60s.

I was admitted on July 20, 1959 after a history of brittle-bone disease had severely restricted my education. I had lost so much education due to injuries that I required private tuition. I also needed the safety of a protected environment. Boarding school, it was felt, would be far too rough and tumble. In the end, my doctors decided QM was the only establishment able to provide me with the best of both worlds.

I was reluctant to leave home and my parents promised, if I was unable to settle, I could come home after two weeks. I stayed for nearly seven years and had the happiest time of my life.

When I arrived on that warm summer's day in 1959, I was far from mindful that I was representing the first post-war youth of Britain. It was a very different world to that of today. I am not going to say the summers were longer and hotter (the summer of 1959 was decidedly mediocre) but the atmosphere of life was very different.

Harold Macmillan's "You've never had it so good" was the neologism of the day, but to this young lad, in the midst of private turmoil, the validity of the phrase seemed highly questionable.

My first years were spent on Ward D8. Sister Ford was in charge and she was the quintessential ward sister. Buxom and fiery, but with a heart of gold, she was on top of all situations at all times.

Sister Ford possessed a strong puritanical streak and insisted grace be said before and after each meal and prayers at the close of day. She would stand, Peggy Mount-like, at her office window looking out on to the verandah, to ensure no one opened their eyes or giggled during evensong.

That puritanical theme was much in evidence at that time. On alternate Mondays, two Bible punchers (this was the term they chose for themselves) would give of their own free time after work to talk and read the scriptures to us. Their names were Mr Giles and Spiller. Mr Giles was tall and suave and looked very inch a preacher; Mr Spiller was shorter and stockier and had led a checkered life before being saved. Time and again he would beg us kids not to travel the path of Satan he had trod before turning to the Lord. He was a true born-again Christian and both were sincere in the beliefs. The seeds of their words deserve to have fallen on fertile soil.

There were many such people who gave freely of their own time. Another was a Mr Chapman who gave of his Sunday evenings to visit the wards with a sack fullsof books, all in pristine condition. These he sold for a pittance (about 1d each) and so it was hardly a flourishing side line he was running! We took all these kind and dedicated people very much for granted.

There was also a flourishing Scout movement which held meetings after church on Sunday mornings, and a stamp club run by the Revd. Edward Noel-Cox, with whom I am still in contact.

As will by now be deduced, our days were ruled by a strong moral theme. We were encouraged to read Children's News (now sadly defunct), but the watching of Emergency Ward 10 on ITV, then very much in its infancy, was strictly taboo. I have to say that I really never understood why. The music of Cliff Richard, then just breaking onto the pop scene with his first big hit Living Doll, was also deemed to be the end of civilisation. In my mischievous moments I find myself wondering how the music of Madonna would have been received!

However, not all showbiz stars were seen as a threat to our morals and among the people I got to meet were Roy Castle, Stratford Johns, Richard Hearn (Mr Pastry) and the ventriloquist Ray Allen.

Ken Bates, the school's art teacher, was quite a celebrity in his own right, and was commissioned to paint portraits of Pat Phoenix and Stratford Johns. At the time, Pat Phoenix was about the hottest property around as her portrayal of Elsie Tanner in Coronation Street, and Stratford Johns had found lasting fame as Barlow in 'Z Cars' and 'Softly Softly'. Sadly, Ken Bates died suddenly and prematurely within a year or two of my leaving the hospital.

Another teacher to whom I owe much is Ron Michell. It was he who surveyed my education wreckage and worked out a goal-plan aimed at skills that were most likely to find me employment. These were typing and English. This was a brave decision, because we were very much into the comprehensive era of teaching and the urge to give me a crash course in all the subjects in the curriculum must have been overwhelming. But Ron Michell wisely reasoned it was pointless my learning French before I could speak English.

I was sent to Miss Nicholls' class and under her tuition learnt to type. It was a great disappointment to her that I failed my exam, but on the day my nerves got the better of me.

In 1962, I was moved to Ward D2 where I met a boy called Nabile Shaban. He, too, suffered with brittle-bone disease, but overcame his handicap to such effect that he became an actor and has had a number of big roles on television. Perhaps his biggest was as Davros in BBC1's Dr. Who. His rise to fame is truly worthy of the highest accolade.

The one recurring theme to strike me over the years was the dedication of the staff. It was more than a job. It was a vocation. A number of the senior staff were war widows. The day-to-day running of the hospital and school had replaced what would have been home and family. It would be unkind to wish a return of the circumstances which brought about that dedication, but there can be little doubt it was to the benefit of the patient.

I ended my and six and three-quarter year stay on Ward C7. Sister Ford was still in charge and, with the encouragement of all the staff, I had been fortunate to find employment with a newspaper of sporting interests. I was discharged from Queen Mary's on December 23, 1965 and began work on January 17, 1966.

There can be no doubt as to the role Queen Mary's played in my rehabilitation. To the medical and teaching staff I owe a big thank you.

LOUISA CLARK

Louisa is seen here holding the medal that she was awarded for winning the SUTTON SCHOOLS CROSS COUNTRY CHAMPIONSHIP over 3/4 mile at Carshalton in March 1993.
Louisa was a patient at Queen Mary's in May 1992.
She was then 9 years old.

LIFE AS A PATIENT IN A CHILDRENS' HOSPITAL IN THE THIRTIES

by Elizabeth Down.

At the age of twelve years, I was told that due to the effect of infected arthritis, I had bilateral ankylosis of my hip joints, and I would not be able to walk again. My father decided not to accept this verdict until he had consulted other medical opinion. He was fortunate to meet an orthopaedic specialist, who was of the opinion that with a series of operations, he could make it possible for me to walk again, although I would always be lame.

So on June 4th 1930, I was admitted to the largest childrens' hospital in the country. It had one thousand beds. Except for short intervals, at home, I was there for three years. Because it was a L.C.C. hospital, and I lived in Surrey, my father had to pay three pounds a week, and the money had to be backed by a guarantor.

The first impression I received as I reached the hospital was a large notice stating Metropolitan Asylums Board. There was a mile long drive up to the reception ward; here I was fitted with white canvas shoes, which made me think I was going to be allowed to get up. I was then wrapped in a red blanket, labelled with my name, and put in a van to be taken to my ward, which was called D.I. There were thirty children on this ward, all lying flat on their backs, or on tip-up beds, which meant that the weight of their bodies kept their hip joints stretched. We were tied to our beds, which were on fracture boards, by restrainers which went over our shoulders and tied under the bed; we had no pillows.

All treatment took place out of doors, winter and summer. We were often cold, and the only comfort we were allowed was what was called a next-to-patient-blanket. This was a small blanket which we could hug close to ourselves. Incidentally few of us had colds, and I seldom have one nowadays.

The only time we were taken indoors, was if we had a raised

temperature, or the weather was foggy.

In bed we were issued with a garment called a shirt, this was made of twill, it had long sleeves and no back, and was tied at the neck with tape. I discovered that the canvas shoes which I had been fitted with were to be worn in bed; this was to keep our feet in shape.

When we became 'up' patients, we were issued with a flannel vest, tied at the neck with tape, a pair of twill combinations, with a flap across the back; on top of this were a pair of navy serge combinations of the same design. To complete the outfit we were given a navy serge pleated skirt, that had been laundered but not pressed, and a navy woollen jersey, black woollen stockings and black surgical boots; nothing was provided to keep the stockings up, so I tried to keep mine up with white tape.

I was so thrilled to be up, that I was quite unaware of what I looked like..... my parents have since told me that they had difficulty in not crying when they first saw me up and dressed in this garb.

Our diet consisted mainly of the following.....

Breakfast, served at 6 a.m., Breakfast Sausage, with bread and butter and a mug of cocoa; sometimes a kindly nurse would fry the sausage for us.

Elevenses, served at 8 a.m., was a mug of cocoa.

Dinner, at 12 noon, this was nearly always mince and mashed potatoes, followed by boiled rice, except for Sunday, when we had sausages, followed by plum duff, even now I can still remember how it stuck round one's mouth.

Before meals were served, we were provided with a diet cloth; this was a large kind of serviette. The food was served on thick aluminium plates, and drinks in thick aluminium mugs. The mugs were far too hot to put to one's lips, until the liquid inside was nearly cold.

In the toilets, instead of toilet rolls, we had out of date railway handbills, tied together with string.

The chief orthopaedic surgeon, specialists they were called in those days, could only perform his operations after 8 p.m. due to other commitments. Because of the anaesthetic, we had to be starved all day, and only allowed barley sugar to suck.

The visiting was restricted to once a week, on Sunday between 2 and 4. Due to the poverty of the thirties, many parents would walk the fourteen miles from London to visit their children.

On one special occasion, when Queen Mary visited the hospital, we were issued with attractive bakelite tea-sets, and colourful bedspreads, which were promptly taken back after the visit.

Birthdays were celebrated by the nurses mixing a large fruit salad in an enamel bath.

Despite all this, the medical treatment was excellent, and the surgeons and nurses worked unsparingly, and today, although I am still disabled, I was able to marry, and have two fine sons.

All this took place before the National Health Service was envisaged.

MEMORIES FROM 1941

Thousands of young patients pass through the wards and nursing care of Queen Mary's Hospital for Children in Carshalton. But it's not often that staff are reminded of the impression the place leaves on the youngsters...

But it certainly left a strong impression on one small boy called John Gibbs, who was a patient back in 1941.

In a recent letter to the hospital John and his memories of German Measles knocked spots off the thoughts of some nurses and doctors who honestly didn't believe the patients cared.....

His letter said: "When I recovered I was supplied with hospital clothes - grey shirt, pullover and socks, a red and black tie and a belt with a snake buckle. The girls fared better - they wore blue and white or pink and white dresses!

We did needlework and games as well as reading and writing in the hospital school. The visit of a big top and circus to the hospital was a great event but the most exciting thing was when a German plane was shot down on the farm behind the hospital and two German pilots were taken prisoner. After 27 years I still have happy memories of the care, I received from the doctors and nurses."

Reproduced by courtesy of
Surrey and South London Newspapers

POEMS by Dorothy Anderson
A former Patient

Printed by kind permission of Dorothy Anderson
from her book "Rainbows Through the Rain"

Thank you, Lord.

Lord, Thank you for today,
My home, my friends, my school, my play,
So many lovely things to eat,
A tale to make my day complete.

For fun, and laughter, joy and tears,
Of memory lane right down the years,
For thoughts of home, the fireside glow,
While winds around the house did blow.

For days of work and hours of ease,
The washing blowing in the breeze,
Relaxing in a TV chair,
For sacred things, the times of prayer.

For Sunday School, and Church, and God,
Record the way our fathers trod,
For Jesus Christ alive today,
The only Life, the Truth, the Way.

Love

Without it, nothing could exist,
No earth, no sea, no air,
No sunlit height, or shades of night,
No life at all be there.

It is so patient and so kind,
'Tis never proud or rude,
It takes the attitude of mind,
Which always sees the good.

It bears, it hopes, believes all things,
For it will never die,
The friend of beggars and of kings,
'Tis written in the sky.

LOVE is the centre and the soul,
Of every living sphere,
Love helps, and heals, and makes men whole,
Wherever it draws near.

It came to earth in human frame,
Those centuries ago,
It healed the sick, the blind, the lame,
Great mercy it did show.

For LOVE revealed itself supreme,
In Jesus Christ, God's Son,
He is the Life, the Truth, the Way,
The only perfect One.

My Heavenly Father

My Father owns the universe,
The galaxies of space,
The sun, the moon, each star that shines,
Were fashioned by His Grace,

The mighty seas belong to Him,
Each mountain, lake and tree,
The cattle on a thousand hills,
The buzzing bumble bee.

Why should I fret and fuss so much,
When He is in control,
Not only in the elements,
But in my heart and soul.

For if my Father owns all things,
And He's a millionaire,
I've only got to come to Him,
And prove His love through prayer.

The stars they speak to me of Him

The stars they speak to me of Him,
His majesty and power,
I see His wondrous handiwork in every tree and flower,
The colours of the rainbow bright, remind me of His love,
Creator of the lowest depths and highest heights above.

The sun reflecting on the sea upon an evening fair,
The blue smoke from some farm ascending like a prayer,
The sheep upon the mountainside with soft white fleece,
Remind me of my Shepherd's care and His promise of sweet peace.

And in his precious work I find, a wealth as pure as gold,
With everlasting treasure, its riches are untold,
For it tells the marvellous story of redemption, full and free,
The wonder of God's love to man, for folk like you and me.

A Christmas poem

Christmas bells are ringing,
Softly through the snow,
Hear the carol singers,
As they on their journey go.

Though the skies be heavy,
And the road seems long,
They still are bright and merry,
Singing their Christmas song.

The star in the East shines brightly,
To guide them on their way,
To that lowly little stable,
Where the infant Jesus lay.

Snowdrop appreciation

Thank You for the snowdrop,
So delicate and fine,
Another emblem of Your love,
To this poor heart of mine.

Thank You for the snowdrop,
Which spells the sign of spring,
The chitter-chatter of the birds,
The flapping of each wing.

Thank you for the snowdrop,
Dressed in green and white,
Reminding us of purity,
The choice of doing right.

Thank You for the snowdrop,
So humble and so small,
Created by that mighty Love,
Embracing each and all.

CHAPTER 3

THE HOSPITAL SCHOOL

By Miss Joan Bower
(see ref. page 98)

In introducing my talk on work in a Hospital School it seems necessary to give a brief outline of the beginning of such work in this country.

The first so called schooling for children who had to remain in hospital for long periods was more of the nature of occupation, to combat boredom and apathy on the one hand or extreme naughtiness and bad temper on the other. Often the motive for appointing a teacher was to help in dealing with obstreperous patients, and the good or apathetic children were overlooked. This plan often worked better than it might have done. If the teacher selected had the right kind of approach she did more than just occupy the children and gave them fresh interests and a new outlook, and in fact educated them so that they sought occupations and interests for themselves. It was largely the work of these teachers which encouraged the more progressive of the Medical Profession to see that education was desirable for children deprived of their normal life and surroundings. It was acknowledged in some cases that the health of the children improved with the provision of education, and that they became more reasonable and manageable.

The first teaching in hospital was usually part time and by voluntary workers. Orthopaedic hospitals and Sanatoriums were the first to establish schools, and this was chiefly in those hospitals run by voluntary bodies. The hospitals at Alton, Oswestry, Leasowe, and Stanmore, have long established schools.

London had its ring of outer London hospitals under the Metropolitan Asylums Board. These were hospitals for London children suffering from T.B., Rheumatism, E.N.T. Eye Diseases, Skin Diseases and Orthopaedic cases. The schools within these hospitals still kept the idea of craft work and occupation well to the fore but qualified teachers were appointed and general education became more established.

The L.C.C. took over the management of its hospitals from the M.A.B., and then the control of the education side was in the hands of the Education department. Under the new control the schools were able to develop more fully, and to enjoy better equipment and facilities and a better understanding.

I started my hospital teaching at one of London's country hospitals soon after the education authority had taken control of the schools. I was appointed because of my qualifications as a Froebel teacher from London's elementary school service. I began work with a group of children on a Rheumatism ward aged 5 to 14 years. I found much of my previous experience and training somewhat useless. I was unable to put my class methods into practice as such, but soon found that the other teachers were working out individual schemes which suited the children well. I remembered the good work I had seen in an adjoining class to mine in a London infant school, that of a Montessori trained teacher, and began to borrow from her experience, and in this way worked out an adaptation for myself. I could not have used her apparatus even if I could have obtained it, the conditions were against that. The children were flat in bed and not allowed to sit up, or in the early stages even to hold a book. It necessitated a study of each child's possibilities both in natural endowments and unnatural limitations. I found that it was often necessary to restore the child's interest in something beyond her illness and the ward, whilst remembering that the Ward for the time being was the centre of her life. To keep in touch with the normal happenings of home, the cycle of nature, and to foster interest in those activities from which the child was debarred seemed to be all important. Somehow a substitute for the normal method of learning and developing had to be found. The child patient must be active minded within his limited environment and thought stimulated by proxy if necessary. A wise and sympathetic Headmistress gave her advice and support, and I was continually learning. The children suffering from heart trouble caused by Rheumatism were often excitable and irritable, but very interested. I found their response variable, but got used to biding my time and seizing my opportunity.

Next to our ward at this time was one of "Babies" as they were called, otherwise the under fives. They were in cots with little or nothing that roused them to active play. They were not "on school". Sometimes a 4 year old was allowed into the schoolroom out of pity for the child's yearning, but this was only when the child was up and mobile. We all decided that if any children needed us it was these little ones and we begged to be allowed to establish nursery groups. I worked with one of the first groups taken under the wing of education and found these little ones either touchy or apathetic. The "sensitive" years spent in hospital call for special help in avoiding chronic frustration, resulting in tantrums or listlessness. There is so much that a hospital child cannot do that she is unable to learn by exploration of the things around, even the normal routine is restricted. Much thought and ingenuity are needed to supply the child with materials that she can and may handle. This first class of mine had been deprived for so long that they took some time to settle into contented play. Frustrations still came their way in the form of treatment, but in the end they learnt to take it in their stride. Now most hospital schools include children from 2 years old and we do our best to provide for them their means of natural growth. This inclusion of the under fives is to me an important development in the history of hospital schools.

In the Education Act of 1944 the hospital school was mentioned under the charter of "Education for the Handicapped Child" and it was made imperative that all hospitals having a percentage of children staying over 3 months must provide special educational treatment. The somewhat conflicting attitude of teachers and nurses towards the child patient makes hospital teaching difficult to establish on the right lines, but patience and forbearance on the part of both the teacher and the nurse will help the child to accept even apparently unnecessary limitations with tolerance and goodwill.

Queen Mary's Hospital, Carshalton, has a long tradition of school in hospital and many of the difficulties have been met and solved, but as personnel and circumstances are continually changing fresh adaptations must be made. Established as a hospital in the country for London children, it now serves as a General Hospital for children with its Casualty department and Acute wards, in which the school has no part. It is true to say that the average stay of children in hospital has been very much shortened by the use of new treatment and drugs. Some of the conditions requiring long hospital treatment have more or less disappeared with improved health services. Others can now be treated by regular attendance at clinics and much preventative work and early diagnosis has lessened the incidence of diseases like Juvenile Rheumatism.

Queen Mary's hospital still has its special departments for the treatment of Orthopaedics, Poliomyletis and Juvenile Rheumatism and its unit for the study and treatment of Cerebral Palsy, and the main part of the school work is carried on in these wards but school is also held in the General Medical and Surgical wards. All wards present different problems, though there are many in common. The age range is often from 2 to 16 years, the backgrounds of the children are very varied, interruptions for treatment, etc., must take place. Added to this is the difficulty of positioning and perhaps a definite handicap or defect. Working on a Rheumatism ward one has to cater for all stages of the illness for patients immobilised for several weeks, others getting up for short periods at different times. All this applies individually and at different rates. All needs must be catered for and the children must be stimulated but not over excited. To observe and follow the needs of an immobile child calls for understanding of the needs of a child not so deprived. The patient cannot or may not help herself to meet her needs in the first instance. The hospital teacher needs to have been trained as Dr. Montessori has said of any teacher to an understanding of the child's need for liberty, and for independence of spirit. She must see that in caring for the recovering child she does not make effort on the child's part unnecessary. Again Dr. Montessori has said that the mind of one who does not work for what he needs but commands it from others grows heavy and sluggish. This is not strictly in context but I think it has its very strong application to the handicapped child, and again, "Needless help is an actual hindrance to the development of natural forces". Unobtrusive levelling of insurmountable difficulties may be necessary so that the child can conquer within its scope. The teacher should know how much a child can achieve and seek to put in his path the timely stimulus. It may be by word or demonstration, through music, language or art. If the child is ready for it and the soil prepared the seed will grow.

Immobilisation is a more serious problem to the young child who needs to handle everything and to be active and busy. The 3 year old

Polio victim who finds himself restricted has to have experience brought to him in such a way that he can explore within his own limits. The blessing is that children so soon adapt themselves, and they find ways and means for outlet, quickly learning from each other.

Actual teaching aids differ from child to child and from ward to ward. Adaptations for one child may not help another but experience helps, and often the child himself will find and point the way. You will understand that the teacher is usually the person available to bring to the child his means of expression and development. She in her turn is handicapped by the need for supplying all materials from her limited storage space, for arranging so that these materials may be handled to the best advantage, and for ensuring that the children are encouraged to maintain the positions important to their good recovery without strain or fatigue.

I hope I have not over stressed the difficulties of the situation. Part of the satisfaction of this work comes from the challenge that has to be met, and the opportunity to achieve the "impossible". The children themselves can enjoy this situation even though at other times the odds seem against them. The child and the teacher can believe that with the closing of one avenue another must be opened, and that if the teacher cannot do what he intended he can find something else that is both interesting and productive. Even a severely handicapped child must realise that he has a duty towards others as they to him. "Happy the child who can come to realise that life is not a matter of bone and muscle or even intellect". There is the spirit which is the essence of life itself and this spirit need not be imprisoned, stunted or maimed. It can grow to full stature and know no limitations.

Details of curriculum are important to the child and he is given as full an education as possible so that he may not find himself at a loss. Common Entrance and School Leaving examination may be taken at the hospital, but as you will see in the photographs and colour films that we have brought, the children enjoy Music, Art and Drama, as well as the more academic subjects. It is our belief that physical disability need not inhibit mental and spiritual growth. Practical difficulties there will always be in plenty, but they must be kept in perspective, and we must strive to help the child patient to be master of himself, and open his eyes to what life has to offer.

School Staff piping band.

PIPING IN HOSPITAL SCHOOLS

by Miss J G Bower

"I never thought I should play real music," said the twelve year old in his spinal carriage. Martin was the last to return to his ward. We had taken the longer route through the grounds and he has drawn his pipe from its case and played one tune after another as we went along. The remark was not just casual and passing, it was inspired by deep feeling and experience. 'Real' music to Martin is anything that appeals to him - folk tunes, classical or modern airs; he plays them all with confidence, and gives a quality to his pipe that is akin to a clear choirboy's treble. It wasn't always so, but this piper had come through the first difficulties that sometimes discourage the would-be piper and disappoint even the sympathetic listener.

At the Ministry of Education Course for the Teachers of Handicapped Children, held in London last September, I was surprised to find that so many teachers had no knowledge of pipe-making and playing, had never even heard of them. I was asked for information and thought that the very best way to give it would be through the pages of our Journal.

If you want the handicapped children in whom you are interested to make and play pipes, first make a pipe yourself, and then make another or show a friend how to make one. Be sure you know how to get a good tone, that you understand how to get the best from your material. Make your preparations very carefully - it needs patience and not a little determination; these mingled with a sense of humour will give you the right start. It is a mistake to expect results in a hurry; this nearly always leads to disappointment. Have confidence in yourself first and then begin with a small group of ten year-olds or over. If you have learnt to make your pipe at a Pipers' Guild Vacation Course or a Class for Teachers you will have gathered some hints about choice of materials and tools and the 'snags' to be avoided. The Pipers Guild was formed to help its members to keep in touch with developments and share the experience of others. The Guild also tries to keep a standard of good pipe making and playing (the Columbia Gramophone Co. has just issued several recordings of pipe music for the Pipers' Guild). It is a pity not to get the best from pipes;,it is so infinitely more worthwhile. It gives you a feeling of awe and wonder when your pipers touch upon real beauty. As one of our most critical nurses said the other day, "I forgive them all their squeaks now." Not all pipers, children or adults, reach the stage of expert playing as a soloist, but most enjoy playing with others and this is a valuable thing in itself.

Does pipe making and playing have any real educational value? From the musician's point of view, music learnt through a pipe that you have made yourself is real and is remembered. The child learns step by step as his pipe progresses. The light and rather delicate tone of the pipe calls for intent listening and seems to increase the child's capacity for intelligent appreciation of music generally. From the craftsman's angle the pipe can give unlimited scope for lessons in the use of tools, accuracy, decoration and finish, and the making of accessories calls for other forms of handiwork.

Although bamboo is very scarce the Guild has approved a tube of beech wood which is pleasant to work and produces good tone. Most important of all the pipe can give to a handicapped child a means of expression that in some measure compensates for his restriction. Both at Horton Emergency Hospital, Epsom and Queen Mary's Hospital, Carshalton, we have felt it most worth while for those children who have to spend a long time on carriages and plaster beds. The pipe is light to hold and comparatively simple in fingering.

If you are interested you can learn about pipe making and playing from any of the Pipers' Guild teachers. There are classes starting in October for any who are in or near London. An enquiry to the Secretary, Mrs Rigg, Meadowrise, Stocksmead Washington, Sussex, will bring details or any other information.

When you do start here's good luck to you! I feel sure that you and your class will find many hours of happiness in this adventure.

Taken from the Special Schools Journal Winter 1946-Summer 1947.

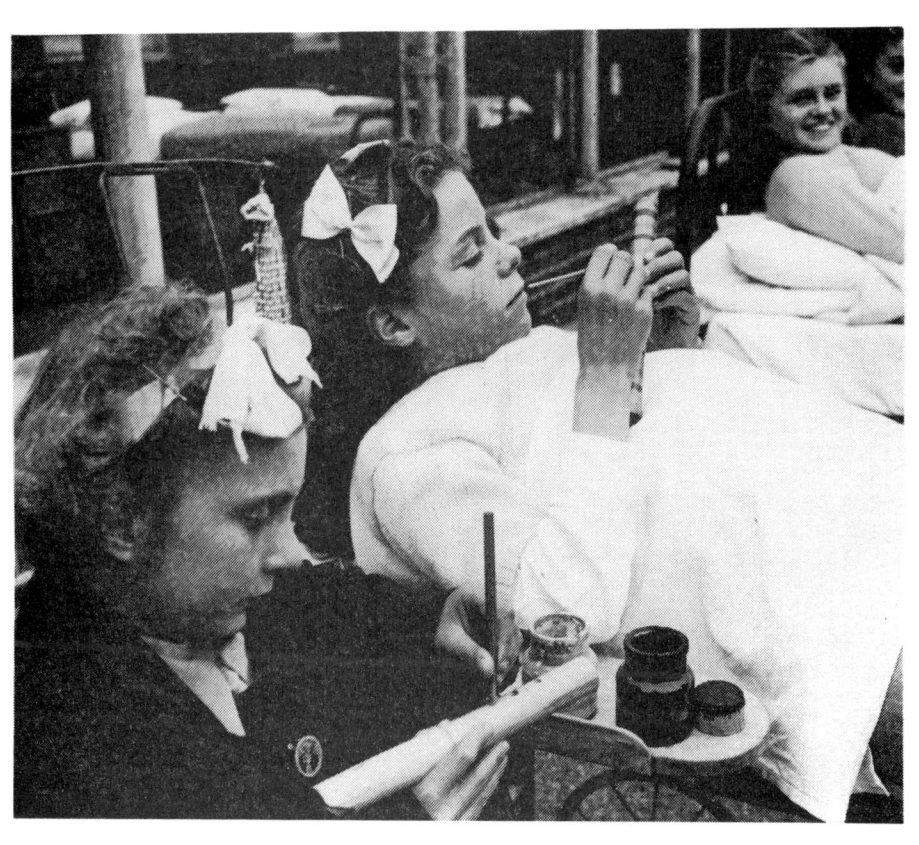

Making pipes for music festival 1947

Staff and patients playing pipes in the court yard.

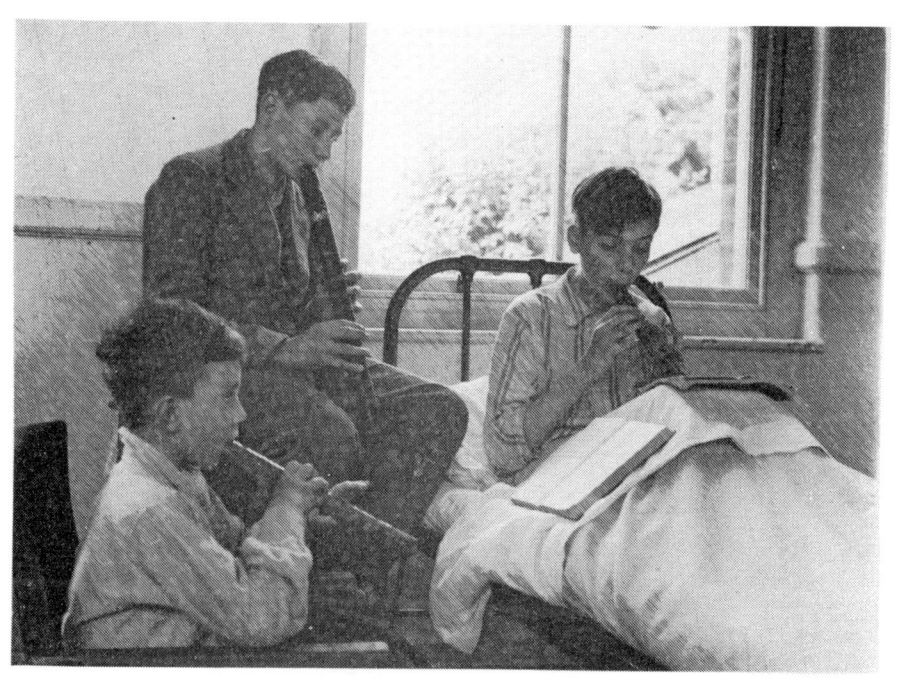

Practice session on the ward.

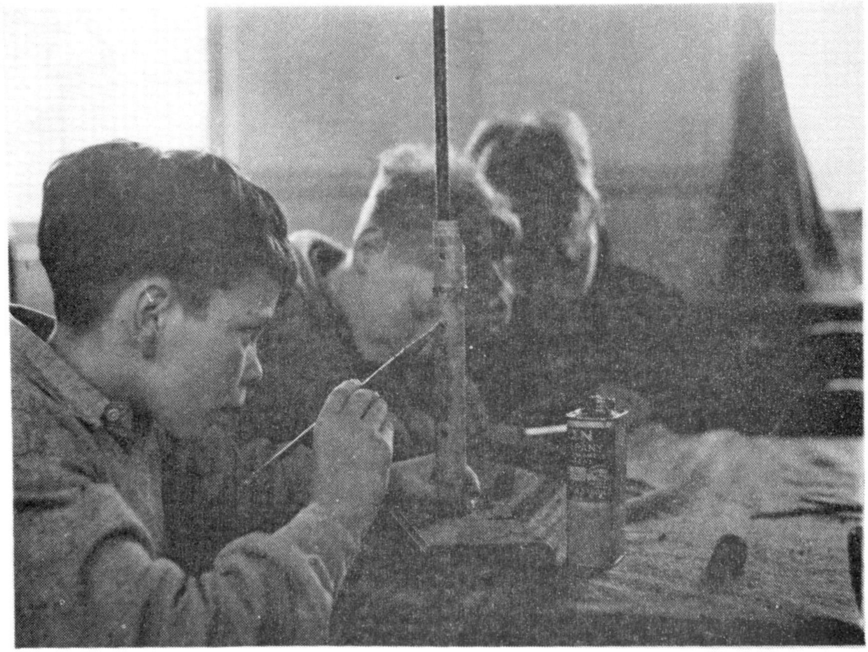

Decorating Pipes

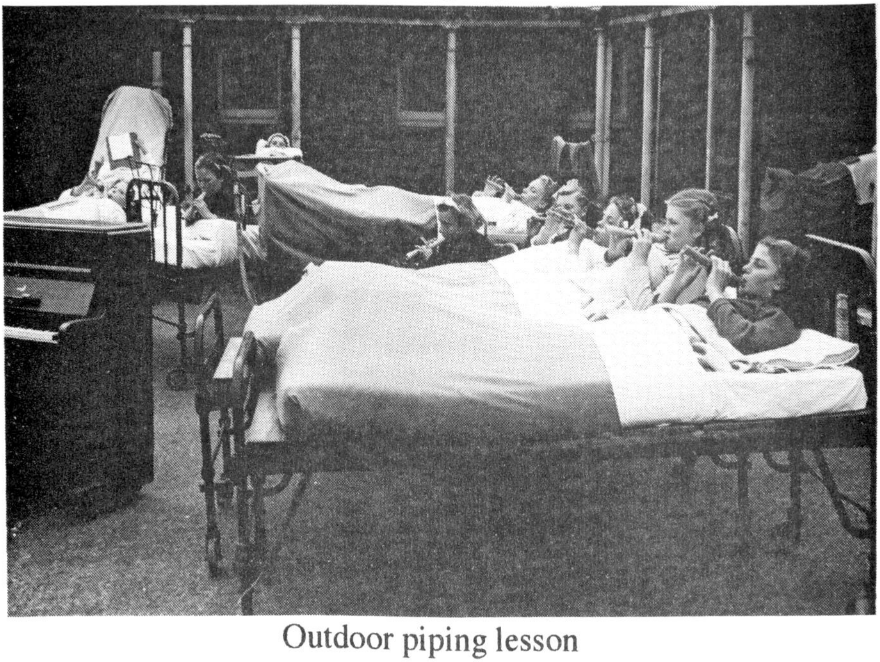

Outdoor piping lesson

QUEENS MARY'S HOSPITAL SCHOOL

Some extracts from the Log Book

May 6th 1912. The school was opened May 6th. 1912. The Staff consisted of two Teachers: — Miss Rogers & Miss Floyd — both Trained & Certificated. Rather more than 100 children were under instruction in the morning & the children of Block B 1 & 2 in the afternoon.

Jan. 1913. In the month of January 1913 the school was re-organised, one more Assistant Teacher was added to the Staff. Miss Webber, She & the Head Mistress, Miss Steward, were transferred from the Downs School, Sutton. The School consisted of about 264 children of all ages from Infants to Standard VI.

Tubercular children
Boys - } Miss S ? name illegible.
Girls - } Miss Rogers

Infant Boys - } Miss Rogers
Infant Girls - }

Boys - Senior} Miss Webber
Girls - Senior}

Boys Junior } Miss Lloyd
Girls - Junior}

In the afternoon the children who are fit to be taught in the following blocks receive instruction as follows:-

A 1 & 2 Miss S
E 1 & 2 Miss S
B 1 & 2 Miss Rogers & Miss Lloyd

March 31st 1913 to April 4th 1913
The new school year began on Monday, March 31st 1913. there were.......children on the Register and 80 are being taught in the Blocks in the afternoon.
    The Matron visited the school on Wednesday morning. Dr. Pugh visited the school on Thursday morning. Average attendance for the week 237. In the afternoon the children who are fit to be taught in the following Blocks receive instruction as follows:-

A 1 & 2 Miss S
E 1 & 2 Miss S
B 1 & 2 Miss Rogers and Miss Lloyd
B 3 & 4 Miss Webber

April 23rd 1914
The following was received:
Metropolitan Asylums Board

Queen Mary's Hospital
    Extract forwarded by Board of Education: from report by H.M. Inspector Mr G A Turner after a visit on March 31st 1914. "The School is doing useful work. The Head Mistress and her staff are well qualified, and as far as the circumstances permit, the children are making satisfactory progress in their studies."

June 24th 1940
Mr Michell's last day on duty as he is called up for the forces and has asked for two days leave before joining on the 27th.
(Later to become Acting Head 1970).
July 21st 1944
School closed at 4 p.m. for summer holiday. Total evacuation of hospital decided and plans being carried out.
July 25th 1944
About 200 children were evacuated to Dryburn Emergency Hospital at Durham.
July 28th 1944
The children have been transferred to other hospitals; the last group left yesterday morning. The school is now closed and the staff will work elsewhere until it is re-opened.
(The school was split between Durham & Knaresborough.)
August 7th 1944
The house "Springfield", Fieldhouse Lane, Durham, was requisitioned by the Ministry of Health for accommodation of the teaching staff.
August 14th 1944
Teaching staff reported at Queen Mary's Hospital to arrange transport of stock and travelling arrangement for those evacuated to Durham.
August 15th 1944
13 teachers arrived in Durham at 5.30p.m.
August 16th 1944
School re-opened at 9.00 a.m. at Dryburn Emergency Hospital, Durham.
November 20th 1944
Mrs Dawson, Head Mistress, has returned to London to visit County Hall and to pack stock at Carshalton.
January 31st 1945
Miss E A Brace on duty to take charge during the absence of Mrs Dawson.
February 8th 1945
(a.m) Mrs Dawson at County Hall
(p.m) returned to Durham

February 9th 1945
Mrs Dawson on duty at Durham at 9.00 a.m.
February 14th 1945
Miss Brace ceased duty at 12 noon.
February 19th 1945
Mrs Dawson ceased duties at 12 noon to take up temporary relief duties at Marlesford Lodge Remand Home.
February 21st 1945
Miss Brace returned to take charge during the absence of Mrs Dawson.
1st March 1945
Junior County Scholarship at Dryburn Hospital. One candidate - Donald Robert Everton.
22 May 1945
Children returned from Durham to Carshalton.
26th May 1945
The teachers hostel "Springfield" was de-requisitioned.
26th May 1945
Mrs Dawson returned from Durham.
30th May 1945
School re-opened at Carshalton

THE HOSPITAL SPECIAL SCHOOL

by Miss Brace
Former Headteacher, who was awarded the MBE for her services to handicapped children.

(reproduced by kind permission of the Hospital and Social Service Journal, first printed 26 May 1950)

The hospital school or, to be more correct, school in hospital, appears to suggest a contradiction of ideas. Surely the purpose of a school is the education of its pupils, while the function of the hospital is the nursing and treatment of its patients. How can these aims be reconciled to each other? Is it a good thing to attempt to educate, nurse and treat a child at the same time, or will he suffer from conflicting ideas? The answer is that the child in hospital needs all three, and would suffer if any one part were left out. The child is a whole entity - body, mind and spirit. The body is sick or hurt and must be cured, but the mind and spirit cannot be set aside while this process is going on. the body may be maimed or ill, but the mind can grow to full stature. Certain children are in hospital for long periods - children suffering from poliomyelitis, from all forms of tuberculosis, from various orthopaedic troubles, from juvenile rheumatism, from diseases of the eyes or skin.

Helping the Child's Readjustment
When they are first admitted to hospital they probably suffer from shock - the child with poliomyelitis finds he cannot stand or perhaps cannot move his arm; the child with a T.B. joint is placed on a carriage; the child with juvenile rheumatism lies flat in bed. In all cases movement either ceases or is very much restricted. All children suffer from frustration at this period; the young ones scream and have tantrums, the older ones may cry with self-pity, or be sullen and resentful. This is the teacher's first task - to help the child to adjust himself to his new life. During this period he is probably having intensive therapeutic treatment, and he will not give much attention to lessons. but as treatment becomes a matter of routine, then he should have as normal a school curriculum as possible.

Children in hospital soon become adjusted; they see others like themselves; they see those who were in before them, getting up and walking, and finally going home; and they have every hope of following on in the same way. They usually become keen on lessons, for they don't want to go back to their own schools and find themselves at the bottom of the class. They will have respect for definite school hours, and a teacher who makes them work at their lessons.

The Academic Subjects

I would give academic subjects first place in the curriculum of a hospital school - from the beginnings of reading and counting to the full syllabus of the higher school examinations. There was a time long ago when nearly every lame boy was expected to learn shoe mending or tailoring, and every girl was expected to earn her living by some form of needlework. Parents now have every confidence in the hospital school and willingly entrust their child's education to the teacher. So side by side with medical attention and treatment, education goes on. The teachers knows that the child is in hospital to be cured; the doctor knows that an unoccupied mind will hinder his work on the body; the sister has learned to look upon the hospital school as a blessing, for it helps to make a happier and more contented patient.

Now to get back to the curriculum. It should approximate as nearly to the normal as possible. All academic subjects taught in the ordinary school can be taught to children in bed, on carriages or frames, or in wheeled chairs. Bed tables, book supports, writing aids, can be adjusted to suit individual needs, I have seen a boy do all the papers for matriculation while he was lying flat on his back; all the apparatus he asked for was a light board he could hold in one hand and the papers to be clipped to it.

Whatever the child's position, it is never used as an excuse for not doing lessons, and the children very quickly adapt themselves to their new conditions. Catherine, aged eleven years, was on a carriage at an angle of 45 deg; she was busy writing when a visitor asked her if it took long to get used to working upside down. "I should think it did," said Catherine, "Quite two days".

The Teaching staff 1948

General Knowledge

Reading and arithmetic will of necessity be taught largely by individual methods. The children come from a variety of schools, they are of varied ability and attainments, and often the age range in a ward is very wide. But topics of general interest may be taken in groups; current affairs, home news, nature study, will be enjoyed by all children. A boy about seventeen years old had returned home after a period of some years in hospital. He was joined in a discussion on a topic of national interest when one of his companions said, "How is it you know so much about this? You were in hospital all that time." He realised he owed that knowledge to his teacher, and was nice enough that evening to telephone her and tell her so.

A High Place for Music

So much for reading, sums, and all the "bread and butter" of learning. What of other subjects? I would give music a high place in every child's life, especially during his stay in hospital. It is a fine outlet for his emotions; it sets free his spirit; it is something he can do and enjoy, either by himself or in company with others. Children can sing in almost any position and will be happy to do so, especially if they are asked to "join the school choir" instead of being told they are to have a singing lesson. Bamboo pipe making and playing is a fine musical training; the children begin to play as soon as they have made the mouthpiece; they learn first rhythm, then notes, then airs, and know how to read music. The work on the pipe can be done by a child in bed; the decoration and polishing makes the pipe beautiful and preserves it. Recorders, too, are splendid instruments for bed patients and, with experience, the young musicians can go on to flute, oboe, or other woodwind instruments. It is both enjoyable and profitable to run a school orchestra and a school choir; to get the performers together to give little concerts and to hear good music by visiting players and singers.

Children Love to Act

Drama should also have a place in the school curriculum. Children love to read plays and, better still, to act them. A little dressing up and a lot of imagination will make a success of any play, and will give the children the experience of living outside themselves. A child sitting up in bed feels

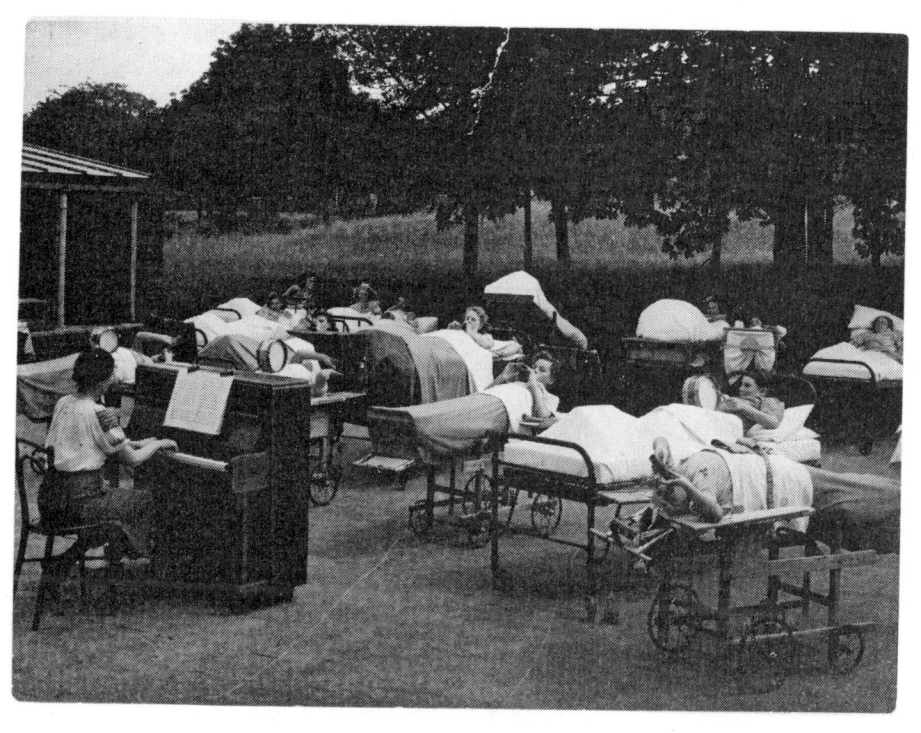

Open air music lesson

A display of art and needlework

regal if he has a cardboard crown on his head and a sceptre in his hand. The children ask for little in the way of properties and scenery, but can make as much of their show as any actor on the stage. Weeks after the children on a ward have given a little play, a child will say to me, "Did you see me? I was a Wise Man and I had the gold box" - and he had been in bed all the time.

Art is of great value to all children, but to the handicapped it becomes one of the finest mediums of expression. A large dust sheet spread across the bed, water pots and paints in a box at the side, or on the bed table, usually avoid any serious upsets. I have seen wonderful pictures painted by children who put into their work all they unconsciously felt or wanted to be. Crafts and various forms of hand work can be very satisfying; a child who has woven a scarf or made a leather wallet feels that he has accomplished something.

The whole tone of the school in hospital should be one of healthy, lively interests. The child should be treated as an ordinary normal school child, and he will usually respond. One afternoon I had taken a party of teachers to see the school. We went to many wards and the children willingly showed some of their work. At the end of the visit one of the men came to me and said, "I didn't want to come here today; I thought I should be depressed. On the contrary, I have never before spent such an exhilarating afternoon."

Enjoyment of Life

The teachers aim to make their pupils feel and act as ordinary boys and girls. If a child is disabled there is no reason why he should be disabled in mind. If the physical enjoyments of life are denied to him, then he must learn to enjoy life in the spirit. Happiness is the keystone on which to build. A happy child is not frustrated, selfish, undisciplined or aggressive, but he passes gladly along from stage to stage until he reaches full stature of mind and can take his place in the world as a thinking, responsible man.

MY OWN TEACHING EXPERIENCE

by Ernest Earl

On completion of my Teacher Training at the College of St. Mark and St. John, Chelsea. I was appointed Head of Boys' P E Department and Junior History Master at Chipstead Valley Secondary Mixed School, Coulsdon, Surrey. By the time the school closed in July 1969 I was in charge of the History Department throughout the school as well as being Head of Boys' P.E.

With the closure of the school I did some supply teaching in a primary school. In 1971 I applied for the position of teacher at the Fountain School, Queen Mary's Hospital. Due to the delay in processing my application, I began work as a porter on the 7th January 1972. This was a most worthwhile and enjoyable experience.

On the 8th May 1972, I took up my appointment as teacher in the Fountain School. Settling in to a completely new curriculum and daily routine took some time.

For most of the eleven years that I spent in the Fountain School, I taught on the wards. With a lot of co-operation and support from the nursing staff, progress with the children's education was achieved.

Activities varied. They ranged from creative and artistic work in the classroom to music therapy, swimming, film shows, visits to the tea shop, train rides round the hospital, picnics, walks, soft play, and going on outings and being taken on holiday.

Both the medical and paramedical staff and the schoolteachers with their assistants, aided at times by voluntary helpers, worked hard on behalf of the children.

Over the years the number of children in the Fountain School and the Hospital School decreased and in April 1980 the two schools combined under one Head, with over a hundred staff.

On the 28th April 1983 I began work on A2, a Surgical Ward. I soon felt at home in my new environment, greatly aided by the support of Miss Muriel Taylor - Headteacher, Mrs Rosalie Cook and the ward staff, especially Miss Elaine Lawrence, (Director of Nursing Services).

After a month on A2: B2, Medical, and B3, General Surgery, were added to my timetable. For one short period I also taught on the Children's Ward at St. Helier.

The daily programme along with the age, aptitude and ability of the children varied considerably. It was not always easy to grapple with the needs of the children or the situation.

I would like to pay tribute to all the children of Queen Mary's Hospital. They were wonderful. Extremely brave and courageous in the face of adversity. Their example has left an everlasting memory with me.

Parents were devoted to their children, often staying up for long hours to support their child, and then helping in the care plan.

The medical and paramedical staff did a first class job. Well motivated and dedicated to the children in their care. They went about their work in an efficient, good humoured and patient manner.

QUEEN MARY'S HOSPITAL SCHOOL
(SOME SIGNIFICANT DATES AND EVENTS)

1912

On the 6th May a school began at the insistence of Dr. W T Gordon Pugh. It was the first school of its kind and became the biggest in the world.

1915

Queen Mary visited the hospital on the 14th May

1919

Miss D Mackie became Head Teacher with a staff of 28.

1921

The staff had increased to 35.

1930

There were 50 teachers and over 1,200 pupils. This was its peak period. The administration of the school was transferred from the Asylums Board to the LCC. Patients were drawn largely from the poorer parts of London. With its reputation for treatment especially of Polio, children came from abroad, including the Commonwealth countries.

1940

The first bombing of the hospital occurred. It was to become the most heavily bombed of all the LCC hospitals.

1942

Miss Mackie (later Mrs Vallance) retired and Mrs F Dawson became Head.

1945

After VE Day the premises were reoccupied, but the war damage meant that the beds were reduced from, 1284 to 840. Mrs F Dawson was promoted to the position of Head Mistress.

July 1948

As a consequence of the National Health Service Act the school was transferred to Surrey County Council.

1951

Miss J Rich became Head but tragically died in a road accident three months later.

1951
Mr H M Tomlinson, The Minister of Education attended the school music festival.
The following is a quote from an article written by Miss Muriel Taylor, a former School Head.
'There were about 750 children on roll in the early fifties, most of them very long stay so that the activities were comparable to those in a 'normal school'. The highlight of the summer term was a music festival. The programme included items from the Staff Choir, the Nurses Choir, the Senior Girls Choir and the Junior Choir. There was also a Senior Boys' band and a Junior percussion band. The most beautiful and impressive sound was from the Bamboo Pipe band some 60 strong, played on instruments made by the pupils themselves as required by the Pipers' Guild, under the direction of Miss Joan Bower. On another summers day a sound like distant thunder filled the air as the wards emptied and every bed was trundled across to the field for the annual fete. Diets were ignored as everyone enjoyed a picnic tea.'
1952
Mrs E A Coventry became Head and stayed until 1968.
1952
During these years the number of sick children declined due to improved child care, especially in the use of antibiotics and the heat treatment of milk.
1958
The hospital and its school were faced with complete closure. It was proposed to transfer the children with Special Needs from the Fountain Hospital in Tooting, London, to the Carshalton site, and completely take it over. The situation was resolved by allocating half the beds to the Fountain Hospital. When the children from the Fountain Hospital were transferred to Queen Mary's, they had their own Head Teacher and staff.
The Cerebral Palsy Unit flourished pioneered by Mrs Eirene Collis. Teachers worked as part of the specially trained team, through the courses held at the Unit three times a year. Other units using these techniques were set up all over the world.

The work on the Polio wards where Sister Kenny's revolutionary methods were put into practice by Mr R Reynolds also enjoyed world renown.

The school was one of the earliest to recognise the needs of boys suffering from Muscular Dystrophy. Their teacher, Miss M Harding, led a campaign where the boys themselves helped to raise money to buy electric wheelchairs.

1965
With the reorganisation of the London Boroughs, the London Borough of Sutton took over the running of the school.

1968
The Head Teacher Mrs E A Coventry retired.

1970
Mr R H Trinder the new Head tragically died in a gliding accident and Mr R A Michell ran the school as Deputy Head for 8 months.

1971 January
Mr C S Holton became Head.

1980 April
The Fountain School and Queen Mary's Hospital school were amalgamated under one Head.

1982
Mr C S Holton retired and Miss M E Taylor became Head.

1984
Miss Muriel Taylor retired and Mr Peter French became Head.

1992 April
Mrs Rosalie Cook was temporary Head from April 1992 until July 1992.

1992 August
The Hospital School was changed in status to that of the Hospital and Individual Tuition Service, with a Coordinator in charge.

1992 September
Mrs Dorothy Jennings became Acting Coordinator.

1993 April
Mrs Dorothy Jennings retired and Mrs Margaret Csillag became Coordinator.

L-R Dorothy Jennings (First School Co-ordinator) Peter French (previous Headteacher) and Margaret Csillag, the present Co-ordinator.

THE FOUNTAIN AND CARSHALTON GROUP HOSPITAL
MANAGEMENT COMMITTEE

Reprint of an article published in the
Group Journal - July 1973

CHERRY TREE HOUSE
by
Dr. Joan C. Wells

reproduced by kind permission of Dr. Wells

By May 1972 builders, decorators, carpet layers finally went, leaving "C Staff Block" empty for its new purpose as a unit for ten disturbed children. A breath-taking display of white blossom on the fine old cherry tree in our little spinney inspired the naming of "Cherry Tree House". Pleasant furnishings, carpeting, carefully chosen playthings, made this a home-like setting in which to work and play and grow a little.

This house and all of us within it are concerned over healthy child life and development, based on the family and seeking to preserve and strengthen a child's own family life. Child psychiatry practised in this way is family psychiatry, and we feel the needs of the family to be wanted and to be "at home" with us are as great as those of the child they entrust to our care. The open lay-out of our two-storey house means no secret places, apart from those the child fashions for himself in play, and families visit us before their child is admitted so that fantasies about the way of life, the staff, and perhaps most important, the other children, can be dealt with, and if admission for the child seems to be the right thing, we can start off on as realistic and acceptable a footing as possible. Separation experiences for both parents and children may indeed be an important part of treatment and have to be lived and worked through by parents, staff and children together. It follows that visiting by parents on an absolutely open basis is our policy and weekend leaves and short holiday periods further link us to home and family. In this way we have been able to admit children as young as three, though most of our group are in the 5-12 year old school age range. Older children sometimes fit well into our setting, depending on their physical and emotional maturity, but in general, adolescents seem to require a more sophisticated milieu, with a range of outside activities and interests which it would be difficult to develop for a very small number of children within the hospital.

As this is a small unit, each worker has a very special value. We do seem to have been particularly fortunate in those who have elected to join our venture, for the great variety of professional skills and experience each brings, nurse, psychologist, teacher, doctor, social worker alike - and the generous readiness to share these with the rest of the group. A basic liking and interest in children for their own sakes, coupled with a certain emotional warmth and stability, to enable one to make diverse relationships, inter-professional, teacher-pupil, etc., etc., in all their multiplicity and complexity, are the essential pre-requisites for this type of work. In such a small group, however, the capacity for sharing, the readiness to face up to inter-professional tensions, and to be particularly flexible in sharing roles or undertaking another discipline's traditional roles, is of particular importance. Thus because of sporadic and irregular parental contact, a social work responsibility may have to be shouldered by the nursing staff for a considerable time, and where a child has particular difficulty in making relationships, any adult may come to fill crucial psychotherapeutic role with that particular child. A high degree of inter-professional confidence and support is necessary to make such a system workable.

"Love is not Enough", Bettelheim entitled his well known book about disturbed children, and those who have not worked with such children and their families may find it difficult to understand what a variety of demands are made and have to be met by workers. We have to be morally and often physically tough, and capable of both hard work and hard, sometimes quick, thinking. The basic needs of disturbed children for affection, toleration, respect as individuals, are more difficult to meet, and the age-appropriate structures of care are more difficult to organise in the disturbed than in the normal child. These children are not angels of light, but have often presented their families with the most trying problems of management, or have family situations posing particular problems for the children themselves. A lack of trust in adults and other children may lead to a great deal of difficulty in relationship formation, to testing out of controls, of their reliability, and of their meaning. Play, the fundamental basis of healthy child life, as is work to the healthy adults, is often greatly disturbed. Our children often have an inability to concentrate, or sustain interest and attention, or they may fantasise, to a frightening degree. The mediation of the adults in play is an essential part of treatment. The richness and variety of the life created with these children depends on the initiative and expertise of our team individually and collectively working in this way, i.e. closely supporting and facilitating.

The routine life of the ward is based on an ordinary child's day, divided into fairly set periods of rest, play, school, activities in the house and outside it in the way of special outings. The fact that we have a schoolroom with its teacher, on the ward, generally enables the most school-shy child to enter a classroom situation right away. Once this has been achieved, consultation between teachers and Head of the Hospital School leads on to placing children with other classes in the school, or in some instances a child may attend an outside school as part of his treatment programme towards discharge from hospital.

We have so far in this milieu been able to accept a wide variety of problems. Habit disorders - encopresis, enuresis, where these do not respond to outpatient care, have formed a high proportion of our younger age group. Neurotic disorders, in particular school refusal, which have also not proved amenable to outpatient management form another group. With the evolution of comprehensive education it is becoming very clear that a small number of children cannot tolerate the large secondary schools and break down at the time of change over, and a period of in-patient assessment of their emotional as well as their educational needs enables us to help advise on future placement whether day or boarding and to support a child and his family through this to a more successful adjustment. A most interesting group has been the children who by long standing behaviour and conduct disorder have alienated themselves sometimes in the home, sometimes in school, sometimes in both. With acceptance, and expectation of reasonable standards of behaviour and conduct over an extended period of time in a stable setting, these children, often with the help of subtle pressure from the peer and adult group, seem able to modify and to acquire a better self image and greater stability. It is however always difficult to assess how quickly such modification can come about and the length of stay on the ward can vary from several weeks to several months. Children with a sensory handicap, such as deafness, have been asssimilated into the group, and there seems to be a particular point here in that in the presence of a proportion of non-handicapped children, they may adjust more realistically. They also bring home in a striking way to all the children the need for the arts of toleration and respect for another individual and his difficulties. Group interaction of the children themselves is a powerful force in such a community as ours, which we also use therapeutically.

Many children with emotional disorder come to the paediatric hospital with physical complaints. Physical illness, such as asthma, may have an emotional component. For these, neurotic child who have headaches, tummy-aches, 'turns' etc., etc., it can be most helpful to be in a milieu where to be "sick" and go to bed is quite possible and acceptable, but not the norm for the group. We have had a number of cases of orthopaedic conditions where recovery has been hampered by emotional factors and have been able to help these, too.

How do we see our future development? This unit is small - we cannot accommodate more than 10 children on a resident basis. We could however expand using day care, and other centres, such as Great Ormond Street, are already proving how well this may meet the needs of disturbed children and their families.

Paediatrics in the seventies will undoubtedly be concerned more and more with the complexity of inter-relationship of physical and psychiatric morbidity in children and we may need a wide variety of clinical settings in which the child and the family can be studied and helped. Already our paediatric colleagues refer us some of our most challenging cases and we have much to learn. We in our turn are trying to develop techniques of management and treatment which we feel will be of interest to all engaged in paediatric practice and may, with research and development, increase our understanding and facilitation of healthy child life in the family and the community.

July 1950
The Minister of Education Rt. Hon. George Tomlinson comes to our Festival of Music

Dr. Agassiz greets Mr Tomlinson

Miss Brace right, the identity of the lady on her right I do not know
Can anybody help??

CHAPTER 4

THE MUSIC FESTIVAL

QUEEN MARY'S HOSPITAL CHORAL FESTIVAL

**While one may not be in entire accord with Addison when he said,
"Music the greatest good that mortals know
Is all of heaven we have below"**

No-one witnessing the first Musical Festival of Queen Mary's Hospital for Children held at Carshalton on Wednesday, November 13th, 1946could have been unaware that it had touched on something extremely rare and fine.

A rapt audience heard separate choirs composed of maids, nurses, sisters, pupil-patients, and teachers compete in song before uniting under the magnetic baton of Mr Meeton to sing for the sheer joy of singing. Probably the standard of musical attainment was not high, but that in itself was a trifle. There was soon an uncommon richness in the atmosphere born of the ennobling power of this universal language of beauty. It had brought these groups together to work for a common end under conditions, desirable and uplifting, and was beyond rational measurement.

The vistas of the mind are limitless and this was an occasion when people had for a time stepped out of the cramping physical, to run barefoot in delightful exploration of the fresh green fields of the spirit.

There had been preliminary work to an extent of which those unfamiliar with the nature and scope of a hospital and school of the proportions of Queen Mary's, can have little conception, but those who had planned and laboured discounted their efforts. Against such a fine achievement all effort was nothing. When one has climbed a mountain and sips of the glory, one does not count the steps of the ascent.

The Festival was wholly a part of the work of the hospital; the process of healing has long been accepted as only partly physical and as the medicine of mind music can and does favourable affect the mental aspect to a considerable extent. Educationally the benefits of music cannot be gauged by examination, they go to make up the fuller deeper and richer life for the individual which is education's aim. Joyful spontaneous creative activity one saw and felt compelled to echo with Bickerstaff, "Tis a sure sign work goes on merrily when folk sing at it."

Taken from the Special Schools Journal winter 1946 - summer 1947.

Copy of Original programme

Queen Mary's Hospital
Musical Festival   13th. Nov: 1946

1. The Chairman, Mr Key, will introduce the choirs.
2. { England   The Children's Choir.
   { The Pigeons
3. Test Piece and Old Winter's Voice.   The Maids' Choir.
4. Test Piece and Elgar's Lullaby.   The Teachers' Choir.
5. Test Piece and Bells of St. Mary.   The Nurses' Choir.
6. Test Piece and Sea Burthen.   The Sisters' Choir.
7. Airs on the Recorders.   Boys.
8. March of the Elves.   The Children's Choir.
9. Adjudication by Dr. Russell and Mr. Rennoldson.
10. The Massed Choirs conducted by Mr. Meeton will sing: —
    (a) O Peaceful England.
    (b) Passing By.
    (c) The Easter Hymn.

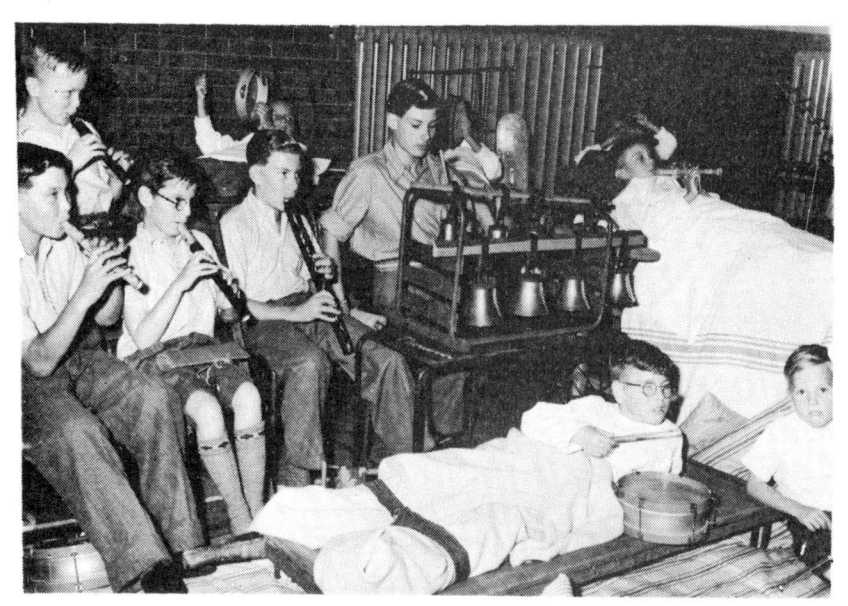

Senior boys' band

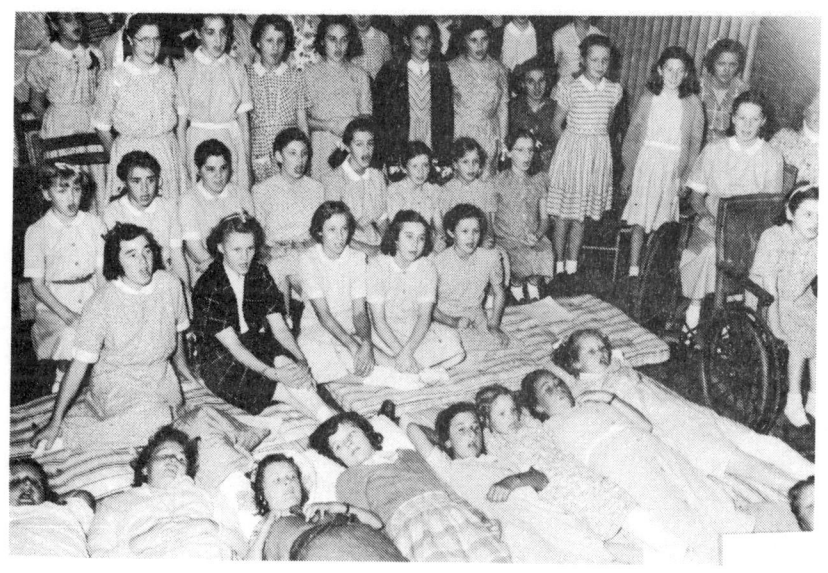

Senior girls' choir 1953.

Mr. Tomlinson comes down from the platform
to speak to the children.

Betty Goodrum a teacher with a group of children

HIGHLIGHTS OF THE SCHOOL YEAR

by Muriel Taylor
Former Headteacher

The aim of teachers was to bring the normality of school life into the hospital situation. The routine of school hours was important but there was also a need, especially for long-stay patients, to organise events which would bring the scattered ward units together as would be the custom in a normal school.

The therapeutic value of music was given its due place in the curriculum so the concept of an annual Music Festival was born. This took place in the Summer Term.

The days of 'family' grouping had not arrived so apart from nursery wards the wards were arranged not only medically but according to age and sex. This made group teaching possible so items for the Music Festival were taught on wards. The groups came together to form the various choirs and bands on the day of the Festival. The programme usually included an infant percussion band, a junior choir, a bamboo pipe band and a senior boys' item. The latter often involved a variety of instruments and provided an amusing interlude. The staff formed a choir and sometimes guest artists performed.

On the day of the festival the school assembled in the Recreation Hall. Some children could walk, others were pushed on their carriages, trolleys or in wheelchairs, and the rest came by van to be carried into the hall by porters. The general scheme was chairs at the back, carriages, trolleys and wheelchairs at the sides and mattresses on the floor for the bed cases. As the children filled the hall visitors were accommodated on the platform.

The performances were of a high standard and honoured by the presence of notable people including the Minister of Education, the Rt. Hon. George Tomlinson in 1950.

A similar event took place at Christmas when the school gathered together in the main hall for a Carol Service. Carols which had been practised on wards were sung to the accompaniment of the bamboo pipe band. Groups of children formed beautiful tableaux to illustrate the Christmas Story.

The grand finale to the Autumn Term was the Christmas Party. Again the children were transported from the wards to the main hall. The younger children usually enjoyed a puppet show, but the older ones revelled in watching their teachers act in scenes from 'Peter Pan', 'Alice in Wonderland', 'Wind in the Willows', and '1066 and all that', as well as fantastic slap-stick comedies written by a member of staff. The play was followed by tea served by the teachers in their costumes and then the trek back to the wards began. By that time it was dark so that was an adventure in itself.

The combined school event in the Spring Term was an exhibition in which each ward contributed a stand showing the work done in Science lessons. There was usually a competition for flower arranging or bulb growing.

Special National events were celebrated by the school. At the time of the Festival of Britain 1951 one of the staff, **Ron Michell**, produced a pageant of the Commonwealth and for the Coronation an historical pageant based mainly on local events. Carriages were transformed into galleons, wheelchairs into thrones, trolleys into Viking ships with the children and staff appropriately attired as they made their way through the grounds to gather on one of the lawns.

These school events enhanced the community feeling especially for those for whom Queen Mary's was their only school or the one which played the most significant part in their lives.

———————————————————

Reference has been made to the bamboo pipe band and it may be of interest to add some notes about this.

One of the teachers, Joan Bower, was a member of the Pipers' Guild founded in 1932 by Mrs Margaret James. The art of making, playing and decorating bamboo pipes was practised in many schools throughout the country.

Joan Bower taught other members of staff and they were then able to teach the children on their wards. Bamboo is light to hold and it was possible for children in awkward positions to make their own instruments. This is done gradually. When the mouthpiece is finished and the pipe tuned, the maker can begin to play rhythms on one note. When the first hole is made he has two notes and when proficient at playing those, the next hole is made and so on. So the skill of playing and reading music comes gradually.

Pipes can be tuned to each other and to other instruments, so that when the children came from various wards to play it was most impressive to hear fifty or more children play as one. Some children progressed to making a consort of pipes and were able to join the staff in part playing and an after school music club was formed.

Playworkers
L-R. Helen, Barbara, Chris, Wendy, Rita

CHAPTER 5

LET'S MAKE A GAME OF IT

Reproduced by kind permission of Nursing Times. This article first appeared in Nursing Mirror on December 22nd 1972.

Play is a natural part of childhood and children in hospital benefit from the provision of play activities, under the supervision of trained play specialists. The play specialists at Charing Cross Hospital (Fulham), are employed by the Save the Children Fund (SCF), working under the guidance of Dr. Hugh Jolly, consultant paediatrician, and Mrs Susan Harvey, senior adviser to SCF Hospital Playgroups; all have had experience of working with normal, healthy children before working with children in hospital. SCF policy is to organise hospital play schemes at the request of senior nurses and doctors, thus ensuring that the project is backed by the hospital staff, from the outset.

Many children undergo adverse emotional experiences in the ward situation, when they are separated from their mothers and families. We, as play specialists, in co-operation with the ward team, and of course the parents, aim to reduce this emotional risk by providing personal care as well as spontaneous and creative play activities. In this way, the child has opportunities for recreation and can freely express his fears and emotions, both hostile and loving. We emphasise the importance of unrestricted visiting to parents and always encourage them to take part in play activities in the ward or playroom. We emphatically are not mother substitutes but work to supplement their care. Play specialists keep records of each child's adjustment to his illness and life in hospital, the type of play situation used and subjective notes on the specialist's own contribution. These observations are discussed with the entire paediatric team at a weekly departmental meeting.

As play specialists, we are the only people never to be called away from the child to perform other duties and are therefore able to create a close relationship with the child.

The paediatric unit at Fulham Hospital comprises a baby and toddlers' ward for 18 children, a ward for children aged three to 15 with 21 beds, and a special care baby unit. Extra facilities include a playroom, two bedrooms for resident mothers and an outside play area. Each ward is run by its own sister.

We work in the older children's ward and in the outpatient department. Another play specialist looks after the younger children's ward and undertakes similar work but with additional emphasis on developmental assessment and the provision of play techniques directed at the stimulation of normal development.

Admission of surgical cases

An important part of our work is the preparation of children for treatment procedures. This includes the preparation of surgical patients for their operations, working in co-operation with the surgeons, anaesthetists and theatre staff. In some hospitals, doctors and nurses do not wish play specialists to do this type of work, in case the child becomes confused by the play specialist being involved in the clinical and sometimes painful side of his illness. However, we find this unrealistic - having established the confidence of the child and his parents, we are in a position to help reduce the anxieties and to answer some of the questions arising from the child's treatment.

We introduce ourselves to the child and his parents when he is first admitted, telling them who we are and what we do. We explain to the parents the importance of play, telling them that we will help to prepare their child for his operation and we will accompany him to theatre, staying with him until he is asleep. The sister or staff nurse has already told us the details of the child's operation.

The child is usually admitted at least one day before his operation which gives us a little time to get to know him before he goes to theatre; it also provides us with a chance to discuss with his parents the best way of preparing him for surgery. The ward sisters help us to encourage parents to be present during the preparation procedure and especially prior to the child going to theatre and on his return. The method and approach varies with the age and temperament of the child.

We try to meet the children when they are first put on the surgical waiting list, usually during their first outpatient visit. This is especially important for children being operated on as "day cases" since these patients are not admitted until the morning of the day of operation.

Preparation

It is important to know from the child or parent, whether he has had any previous operation, how much he remembers and what was his reaction.

Our part of the preparation can take place anywhere, anytime, in the playroom, ward, on his bed or in the reception area. We never take children away from group activities. Other children around may or may not become interested in the proceedings.

We often start by reading with the children one of two books, 'Zozo goes to the hospital' or "Lisa goes to hospital". We keep a "hospital box" containing a small theatre gown; theatre cap and mask; rubber gloves; "nil by mouth" label; syringes; anaesthetic mask; plaster of Paris bandages; plastic tweezers; eye pad and other dressings; and a large teddy bear. This medical kit is always available for spontaneous play and it is left in the ward during evenings and weekends so that the nursing staff can play with the children.

The preparation usually takes the following form:

1. A relationship is usually established between the play specialist, the child and his parents in order to find out how much, if anything, the child knows about his hospital admission and operation.
2. Mother reads 'Zozo goes to hospital' or 'Lisa goes to hospital' to her child, or the play specialist may read the story, at the same time relating to the equipment in the hospital box and, in the case of a young child, dressing up teddy as a patient.
3. Telling the child why he has to wear a "nil by mouth" label. In our hospital this label is pinned to the child's clothing to ensure that no food or drink is given prior to the operation. He is told that he may feel hungry, thirsty and rather cross. The child puts a "nil by mouth" label on to the teddy.
4. He dresses the teddy in a theatre gown while the play specialist explains why it has to be worn.

5. The effect of pre-medication, oral or intramuscular, is explained. Most children have had previous experience of injections, but have not usually had the opportunity of playing with syringes. At this stage of preparation, the child plays the nurse/doctor role; he enjoys being master of the situation and injecting teddy.

6. An explanation follows about going to theatre on a trolley, what the porters wear and where the theatre is in relation to the ward. This is a suitable time to take the child with teddy and his mother for a walk to the operating theatre, at the same time pointing out to the child's mother the canteen where, on the following day, having accompanied her child to the theatre entrance door, she will be encouraged to relax with a cup of tea. The nurse or play specialist who has waited with the child in theatre until he is asleep can find her there afterwards and reassure her that her child is asleep and fine.

7. The child now knows exactly where he is having his operation and that the play specialist will stay with him in the anaesthetic room until he is asleep. This "special sleep" is also explained and carried out by the child on teddy, either by injecting into teddy's arm or by using the anaesthetic mask. We tell children that that they can sometimes choose between an injection and a mask.

8. The child is anxious to know that he will wake up in his own bed in the ward, if possible with his mother at his bedside. He is told that he will feel muddled and thirsty for a while, and that he will only be allowed sips of water. He is also told that this will pass very quickly and that he will soon be up and about again. We explain that play will start again as soon as he feels like it and that he does not have to wait until he is up.

9. If the child is having stitches removed, he likes to know that he will not have to stay in bed until the nurse removes them. This is an opportunity to tell the child that, wherever possible, children are up rather than in bed and that we like them to wear their own clothes rather than pyjamas when they are up. We stitch teddy, the child removing the stitches with plastic tweezers; he then dresses the wound, just as the nurse does. The emphasis on the final procedure is that although it hurts a little after the operation, it is getting better all the time.

Preparing the older child is somewhat different. He often wants to talk about himself and his feelings about the operation, usually sitting on his bed or somewhere quiet. He enjoys looking through the hospital box. Chatting to other children who have had operations can prove reassuring. Both the house surgeon and anaesthetist visit the child and chat informally to him, answering his questions.

From questions such as these, we learn what the children's fears are and are therefore more able to help.

"What will I see in the theatre?"
"Will I go to sleep?"
"How do they know I am asleep properly?"
"What happens if I wake up in the middle of my operation?"
"How long will I be in the operating theatre?"
"Will I wake up as soon as I get back to the ward?"
"Will I come straight back to my own bed?"
"Will my bed be in the same place as it is now?"
"Can I eat and drink when I come back?"
"Will it hurt?"
"Will you come to the operating theatre with me?"
"Can I have the gas mask rather than the needle?"
"Can I have medicine to drink rather than a needle before I go?"
"What if there's a power cut halfway through my operation?"

As well as this preparation we also have "hospital play". The children dress up as nurses and doctors and, by handling the syringes, stethoscopes and other equipment, they can work out their fears and aggressions. They make their own hospital corner in the playroom, thereby playing out the role of doctor and nurse as they see them. At this stage it is useful to sit apart from the group, observing the mode of play and conversation. On one occasion, a child was about to be given his pre-medication injection by the child nurse, but refused to co-operate and left the group. The child nurse got very cross and said, "It's not fair, Timmy won't let me dead him for the operation".

JOE.

CHAPTER 6

THE LATE JOE SMITH

Joe started work at Queen Mary's in 1913. He was employed by a buildings contractor. Soon after this he became a porter.

In the autumn of 1917 Joe joined the East Surrey Regiment at Kingston to fight in the First World War. He went to Crowborough (Sussex) to do his training and passed out as a Lewis Gunner. After basic training the battalion was put on draft for France. His pay was 6d a day (18p a week in todays money).

Joe travelled with his comrades on a cattleship from Folkestone to Boulogne, packed in like sardines, with little food, in atrocious weather conditions.

On arrival at Boulogne they lived in Bell tents, 21 to each tent. They were then sent up the line in cattle trucks, being shelled all the time until they arrived at Ypres. Joe was now nearly 19 years of age.

The soldiers were put in a horseshoe shaped line for 10 days at a time, about 300-400 yards from the enemy. Rest after this meant non-combat duties, e.g. digging trenches.

At 3.00am one morning they saw an Observation Balloon. The soldiers were all lying down covered in mud. About 10 yards from Joe was a shelter. He got under a piece of this, in a state of complete exhaustion.

Within seconds of getting under the shelter a shell dropped amongst them. The blast shredded his uniform, wounded and blinded him. His mates carried him down 50 steps to the Ypres Canal Towpath. Underneath were tunnels. Joe was eventually put on a Red Cross Ambulance with three other soldiers and driven to a railway station, out of gunfire range. They were then put on cattle trucks to Provence.

On arrival at Provence the wounded and gassed were put in marquees and operations were carried out under canvas. There were lines and lines of wounded soldiers. Joe's legs were numb and he was blind. He was fed by soldiers either side of him.

After treatment he was transferred to Boulogne and taken by Red Cross Ship to Dover. Sailing was delayed for 3 weeks because of German 'U' boats in the Channel.

Joe arrived on a beautiful day at Dover. He was then taken by train to Glasgow, where crowds of people were waiting to greet the soldiers. With his comrades he was put into a High School that had been converted into a hospital. They had plenty of visitors and were very well treated.

For 6 months Joe was confined to bed with his legs under a cage. His eyesight gradually improved and he managed finally to get around on crutches.

Everything (except drinks) was free to the soldiers in Glasgow. Women bus drivers did not take their fares, food and trips up the Clyde etc. were provided for them.

After 9-10 months Joe was transferred to Walton in Surrey, and then discharged on a full pension from Kingston Barracks. Joe served his country with distinction.

Unfit for work on discharge from the army he recovered sufficiently well to start work again at Queen Mary's in 1924.

During his time as a porter he worked with Sister Elizabeth Kenny for 3 years. She offered him a job with her in Australia but he declined to go. Joe retired in 1966 from Queen Mary's as a Gate Porter.

He spoke very warmly of Edith Cavell the First World War Heroine. During the Second World War he remembered the advent of V1's and V2's that led to the decision to totally evacuate the hospital).

Joe's story of his time at Queen Mary's is told here. He was 91 when he gave me this interview at his home close to the hospital.

'A truly kind, compassionate and brave man'.

JOE'S STORY

Now the night the bomb dropped, I was on that night then - all the ceiling was down on top of the kids in B8. Cots were blown into the middle of the ward and the cots were touching like that and the heads of people were tangled up like barbed wire. That was with the blast, they were all underneath their blankets in their beds all covered in plaster, the windows had gone and the blackout was going out and all the screams were going out. I said to nurse, "Nurse, have you any salt to throw on that fire?" So I had to splash it out with water because of course we were in the darkness by the fire, but Sister Hope she came running across from the homes with her clothes in her arms saying, "Oh Joe! Is there anything more terrible?!!" "No Sister," I said, "I think everything's alright" Sister said, "You know Joe, I took little Jo Wyman out of the Day Room back into her bed last night and she missed the bomb. She would have had the bomb all to herself; dropped on the Day Room, it did. So she missed it." Sister was crying like a kid... (There was little girl in the ward, blond hair girl, she was about 5 or 6 and I used to take her for treatment down to A7 and Sister said she'd been playing up for quite a long time so she put her in the day room).

It was a hectic night, and we loaded the kiddies up, we put some in the bowl room; some round the lavatories; some in the kitchen, wherever we could lay them and we were waiting to find out what Ward we were going to. So we were going to D5 that's where we were going to take these children - so when we got them half unloaded at D5 someone came across and said there was a time bomb at the back of D5. So we had to take them to F8. We were exhausted by then. So we get all the kids, well we got plenty out there at the finish.

When the children were evacuated, Nell my daughter was coming up with me. She was up at............. with a load of children, she stayed up there for a long while. Now they said to me, "Joe, where would you like to go?" "Well", I said, "I don't know where I'd like to go until I go home and see my wife and see what she says". So I came home here but my wife wouldn't move. I went back and told them so, of course, I had to stay there. I would have liked to have gone to Wales; they had a lovely time in

Wales. Anyway, we stayed here - up and down the shelter - bombs up and down the shelter here - under the ground there. I was of course more in the hospital than I was here.

The whole lot of children went from the hospital - it was absolutely empty. Some went to Knaresborough, some went to Wales, some went to the West Country, all over England and they never came back. The hospital has never been the same since. After the bombs had dropped that night there were loads of coaches coming up the drive - 6 o'clock in the morning - and at 12 o'clock there wasn't a kiddie in the hospital, they'd all gone - in 6 hours. After there would have been about 15 Porters staying there at the ARP. The Council had built that - where the Porters Mess was that was the ARP which was bomb proof. It was an ARP post.

In 1959 the National Health Service Act made it into a comprehensive hospital, when they joined it up together and they brought their kiddies from the Fountain in Tooting. About 300 beds each - each department.

In 1947 when they started to get all the children back in from all over the world it was my job to do their parcels up. I used to get their boots, callipers, from A6, I used to get ENT from D2. I used to get stores work from stores office, samples and all that - that was my job to wrap that up and send it away, I used to take it round to the drugs office at the AD and they used to stamp it and so it went out every night. It was my job to wrap it up and put the address where it was going to in a book I had. That was my job. That was created in 1947 for the National Health Service - I finished in 1966. Worked from 1913 to 1966 in the hospital.

I don't know anyone now that used to work at the hospital.

The Nurses Homes opened in 1930. The Chapel was built before the homes because we used to store a lot of blankets in the Chapel during the War. The Chapel was always open - never locked. I used to help the Padre out a lot with empty boxes - he used to come and ask me for empty boxes.

Dr. Pugh was the first doctor that came into the hospital and the Gate Porter he came from Earls Court, he lived in the Lodge and he was there permanent. He had a doorway made to go back into his living room from the Gate Lodge. Everything that went in there had to be weighed outside the Porter's Lodge on the Weighbridge, but it ain't there now, its been taken up. We had to weigh in all coal, all coal going down to the stoke hole had to be weighed. All coal had to be brought into the Wards and had to be separate. You had a fair busy time on the Gate those days - you had to book teachers in the morning - put it all down in the book - in and out. They came in at 9 o'clock and went about 3 to half-past and they all used to teach their kiddies in the Day Room until they built the Recreation Hall down by where Lollipop is. Dances and Concerts in there too. They've had dances in the Recreation Hall until quite recently - (1990).

You can say that I've seen the start of Queen Mary's till now. You see Case More was the name of the Gate Porter. He came from Earls Court and I used to relieve him at his dinner hour and then he was relieved at 8 o'clock at night and he was there all day. He started 6 o'clock. Of course, he could always go in and out of his living room for a cup of tea.

They were pushed for Gate Porters - they said to me - "Joe, could you manage doing the packing and do 2 shifts down the Gate Lodge?" I said, "Yes". I could do that packing job in my head, I could do that easy. I used to do 2 turns on the Gate Lodge and then drop back on my packing job. I used to be on the Patient Car outside, moving kiddies all over the place - transfers, going to treatment, going swimming, drill all sorts and I used to be on that car and the 3 years I was with Sister Kenny I handled 60 children every day. It's an awful lot of kiddies isn't it? There was about 8 or 9 masseurs and 2 Australians and Sister Kenny - she was a wonderful woman and they all used to do about 8 or 9 kiddies themselves and I used to keep them going so, roughly speaking. I used to take 60 kiddies from A8, B8 and B7 into where the bars were in A7 and they done their exercises and then they used to have the advantage of..........come down about every couple of months and then I used to carry the kids in for the doctors to examine them. That was a busy job.

I enjoyed Queen Mary's, but my ankle got so bad that I asked to be taken off. (That was where I got shot). That got so bad and they sent another fellow up there and he came back the next morning down to the office and he said that there was enough work up there for 2 Porters never mind about one Porter and I'd been doing it for 3 years, but I never went back there any more.

Sandbagging

Devastation of a ward following a bombing raid.

I retired in 1966. I had to go before a committee and I was sent for by doctors and all the heads up in the Committee Room upstairs and all the palaver. I was sent for, for doing Services to the hospital and given a cheque for £25.

There used to be big boys up in C street and there used to be an attendant on C1 and 2, C4 and 5, C7 and 8. They were big boys all waiting to go out to.......... to learn the trade and all that. So there was an Attendant on 3 blocks, 3 wards - C1 and 2, C5 and 6 and C3, 7 and 8 and I used to go relieving them occasionally when it was their day off.

I used to help Dan with his horse and trolley picking up the rubbish - Punch was the horse's name. Dan Doulton was religious - he wouldn't kill a rat he wouldn't. He used to pray for the horse before he left it at night time. Never heard him but seen him kneeling down by the horse. I was delivering one morning in the Winter time when the roads were very slippery - we should never have been out on the streets but round about 7 o'clock Punch went down. I went to him and said, "Let me sit on his head, Dan". He said, "Alright Joe, with the help of the Lord we shall manage." With a bit of harness broken and the shaft broken we got him up alright and we tied some sacks around his feet. No, we shouldn't have been out that day! In the middle of winter we'd been coming down the main drive came across E Street and skidded right into the garden. Punch was alright, nothing to speak of, but that broke his heart when he had to get rid of that horse. He had to pack up because Dan was finishing and they had to get rid of him and he was sold to a man up in Woodmansterne to pull his pig cart but I expect old Dan used to go up and visit, but Dan didn't live too long after. On Sundays he used to go up and see the horse on his day off.

When Dan had his fortnight's holiday I used to do his job. They used to have a contract that all the clinker out of the stoke holes used to be thrown outside, out in the yard, and when the contractors couldn't come and get it I used to have to keep it clean.

You know where the Stanley Road Gate is, well you know where the wood is on the right hand side, there used to be a pond there - that's why it disappeared. Ah, some happy days, but there you are, some good days and bad days - there you are, you don't have good times in wars. You see

I was born about 18 months too soon - I shouldn't have ever been in the war - terrible things going on over there everywhere was smashed down.

You try and find that *photograph, it's in the hospital still and there's my name and address on it and I gave it to Dr. Ward and when he retired he said he'd given it to a Dr. Morry and it's in his ward, but whether Dr. Morry is there or not I don't know. Try and find that photograph of all the staff in the early 20's, the first photograph that was taken with all the staff. That was the doctor, who we didn't know whether he was a man or whether she was a woman doctor, but she was one of the first to ever attempt to swim the English Channel.

I had a wonderful time there; I used to love Christmas there - we never had no time off for Christmas; we used to get well treated there at Christmas time with the staff, with the nurses and sisters - plenty of booze, plenty of cigars, plenty to eat.

One set back I had at Christmas was when I was with Sister Kenny. There was a Nurse in A8, I think she had Polio or something like that, she was a nice girl. This was Christmas time and her people were very well off so she used to provide everything for the kiddies on A8 that they could buy for them and everything was loaded with plenty of everything for the children and they were going to have a good Christmas. I go there on the Christmas morning and she'd died in the night. That was my worst memory.

There you are, our ups and downs, there were good times and bad times, but there you are, wars disturb everything.

N.B. **During the First World War Joe was wounded (blown up) in Belgium and was brought back on a Red Cross ship and then transferred to Glasgow for treatment
* The photograph was hanging up in Dr. Meller's office.

**** Omitted words due to unclear meaning on tape.

CHAPTER 7

The Friends of Queen Mary's Hospital For Children and Orchard Hill

The Friends, as presently constituted, was formed out of two existing Friends' groups, that is to say, the Friends of Queen Mary's Hospital for Children and the Friends of the Fountain Hospital. This amalgamation took place in 1959 with the move of the Fountain to Carshalton. The new joint body took the name of one of its founding members - The Friends of Queen Mary's Hospital for Children.

The two founding groups had been formed some years earlier and had been active charities supporting their own hospitals. Queen Mary's Friends had already established its annual fete, which is still going strong, and has already become a notable local event. They, and the Fountain Friends, had been active in support of their hospital's opposition to the early proposals for their closing down and moving. The Fountain Friends had been involved in forming the National Society for Mentally Handicapped Children (now MENCAP). They had also taken a leading part in acquiring Osborne House at Hastings, originally a holiday home for Fountain residents and which is still going.

The membership of the new amalgamated Friends was formed out of the memberships of its constituent memberships and its Committee out of the two Committees. It carried on the work of supporting the new comprehensive children's hospital in the same way as the individual Friends had been doing for some years. Its aim was to encourage and direct the support of the public in the work of the Hospital and to generate funds with which the resources of the hospital service could be supplemented. This was originally seen as providing additional amenities but, as time has gone by, there has been an increasing need for donations of medical equipment, athough the provision of amenities has gone on in parallel.

The establishment of Orchard Hill as a separate unit, caring for mentally handicapped patients, led to the Friends changing its name to "The Friends of Queen Mary's Hospital for Children and Orchard Hill" thus emphasising its commitment to both sides of what had been the

Fete day 1948

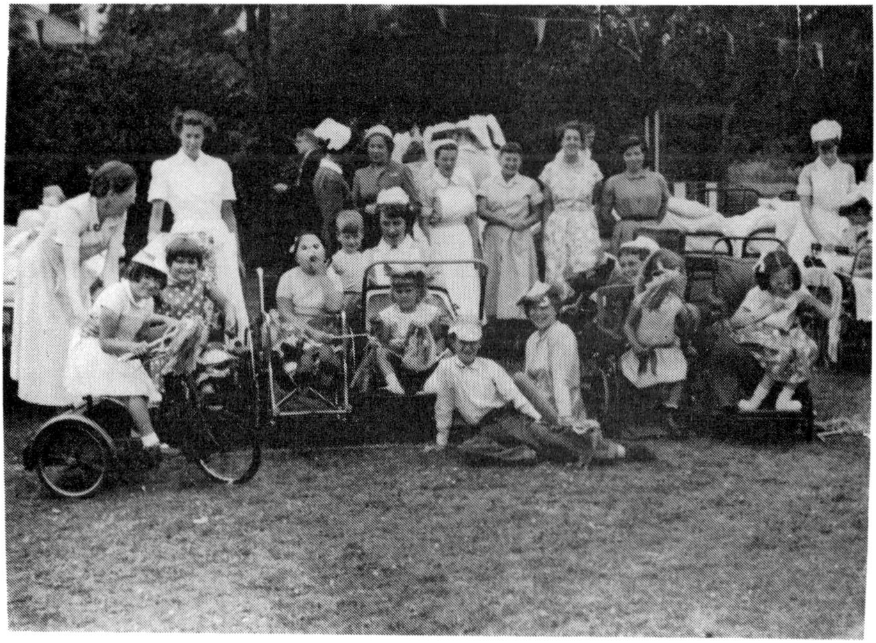

Hospital fete 1949

Having fun on fete day.

comprehensive Queen Mary's. When ultimately the two parts were split and sited in different places it was decided that the Friends should continue to support the individual units and their associates which, although members of different NHS Trusts, had originally been the parts of Queen Mary's and Orchard Hill. The Friends has for some time been a registered Charity.

Support for the Hospital has continued over the years and in the last few years the value of gifts to wards, departments and bungalows has been about £60,000 a year.

The emphasis on medical, therapeutic, educational equipment and furniture has been growing although support is not restricted to this. The medical equipment has included such items as ultra-sound scanners, a blood gas analyser, a gastroscope, accident trolleys and incubators. On the educational, therapeutic side, equipment has been provided for activity centres, both outdoor and indoor, as well as for the Further Education Centre and the School. Specially designed vehicles have been donated to facilitate mobility. To ease the comfort of patients and residents, special beds and baths have been given; also furniture and furnishings for bungalows, wards and for parents' accommodation. This list is by no means exhaustive but it does give some indication of the type of support that has been, and is, given to the Hospital and Orchard Hill. As mentioned earlier, as well as these basic gifts the provision of the more obvious amenities such as televisions, audio and video equipment has been continued. There have been regular Christmas gifts and the support of firework displays by the Round Table yearly.

A canteen has been maintained from the earliest days, as was a shop in the nurses' residence. The canteen was initially held in the Recreation Hall every Sunday, then in the gate lodge which had been rebuilt at the Friends' expense. The service was then extended to a daily basis. Finally a special building was purchased and located near A & E. This was called the Friends' Centre, which continued to give a valuable daily service to patients, parents and staff. On the Hospital's move this building was bodily transported to the St Helier site where its service continues.

Since the move of the Friends' Centre a Log Cabin has been built at Orchard Hill to give residents and visitors somewhere to rest and have a cup of tea.

Throughout, these valuable services have depended on the support of volunteers whose efforts have also considerably boosted the funds.

Support has been given to the miniature railway which has been a feature of the Hospital since the Friends' amalgamation. The Friends have provided locomotives and rolling stock as well as financing maintenance work.

The Friends took a lead in building up and maintaining Pets Corner, as well as funding rides for residents with the Diamond Riding Centre for Handicapped Riders.

In the mid-1970's it was decided to provide a holiday home for residents and, after a fund-raising campaign, three caravans were purchased in 1979 and located at Selsey on the Sussex coast. These were used extensively until the mid-1980's when changing holiday requirements reduced the demand for them. They continued to be used but were gradually sold, the last one being disposed of in 1994. They nevertheless provided holidays for some fifteen years; the residue of the initial fund raised still supports holidays for residents taken elsewhere.

A most important activity of the Friends, in fact probably the most important, is the raising of funds to support its work.

The annual fete has been mentioned and although its earnings have diminished a little, in common with most Charities' fund raising activities, it still forms a major source of revenue, as well as being a very well-known local event.

A continuing and most valuable source of funds has been the donations from the Carshalton Pantomime Company and its costume department, over the life of the present Friends, and even before that. The Company has also been active in the Friends' other fundraising ventures.

Mini-coaches have been operated to raise money for the Friends at their own and other events.

Other fund raising ventures over the years have included antique fairs, race meetings, an assault course, transport extravaganzas and vintage car rallies.

The Friends are also dependent on the subscriptions, donations and bequests which they get from the membership and other supporters.

CHAPTER 8

HISTORIC AND MODERN PHOTOGRAPHS

History in pictures
Who's who??
if anybody recognises themselves will they please contact me
(Ernest Earl on 01737 822661)

123

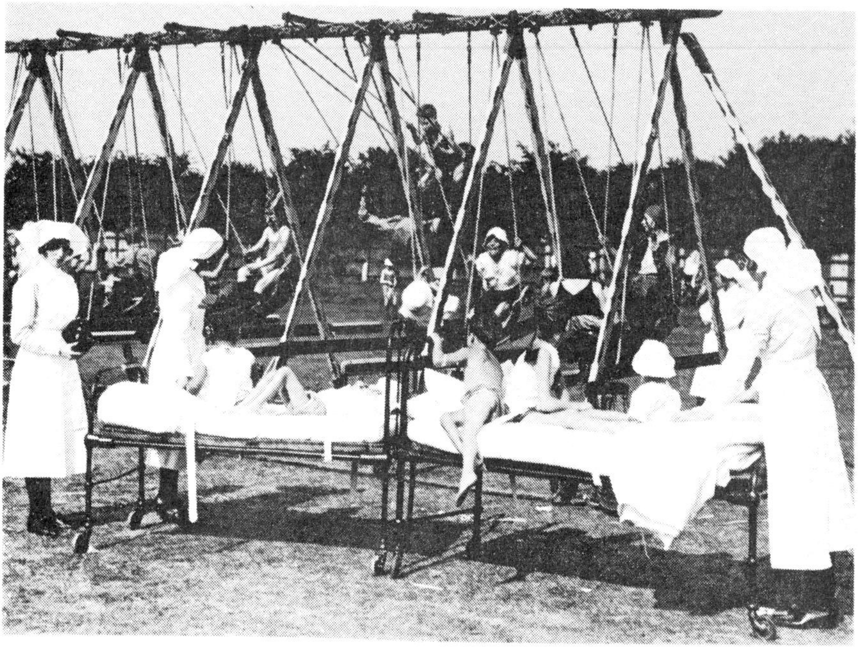

124

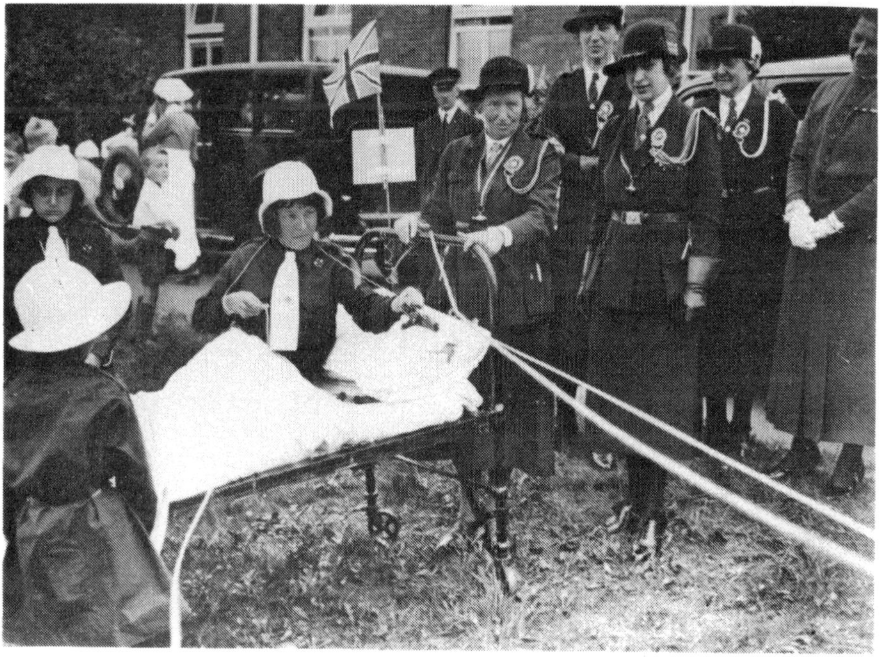

125

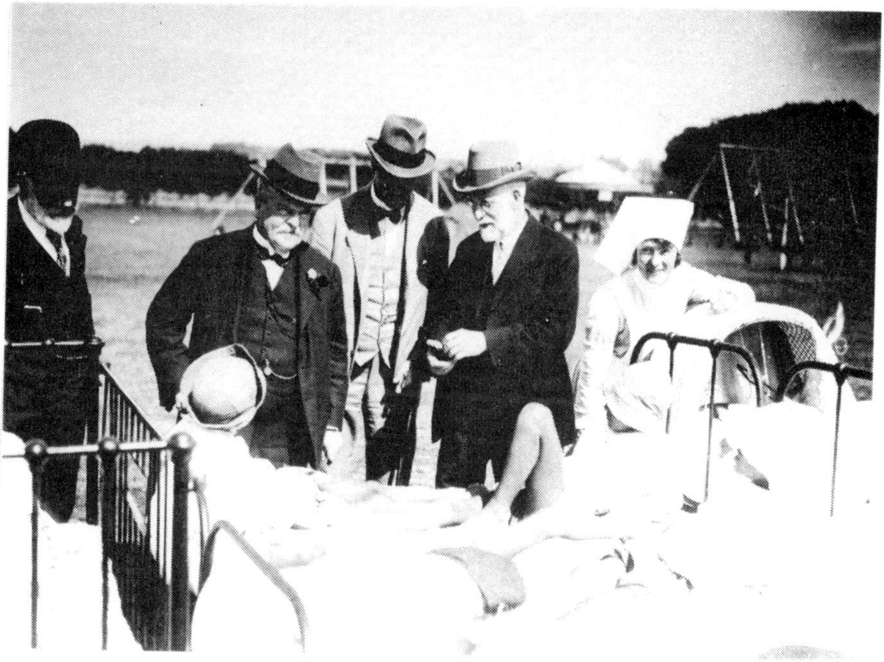

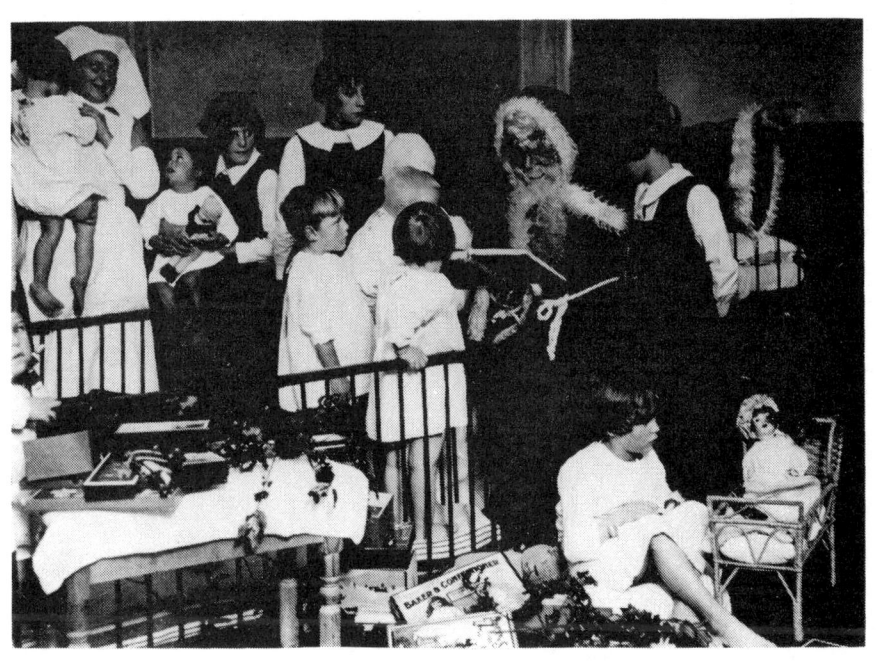

Happy times at Christmas

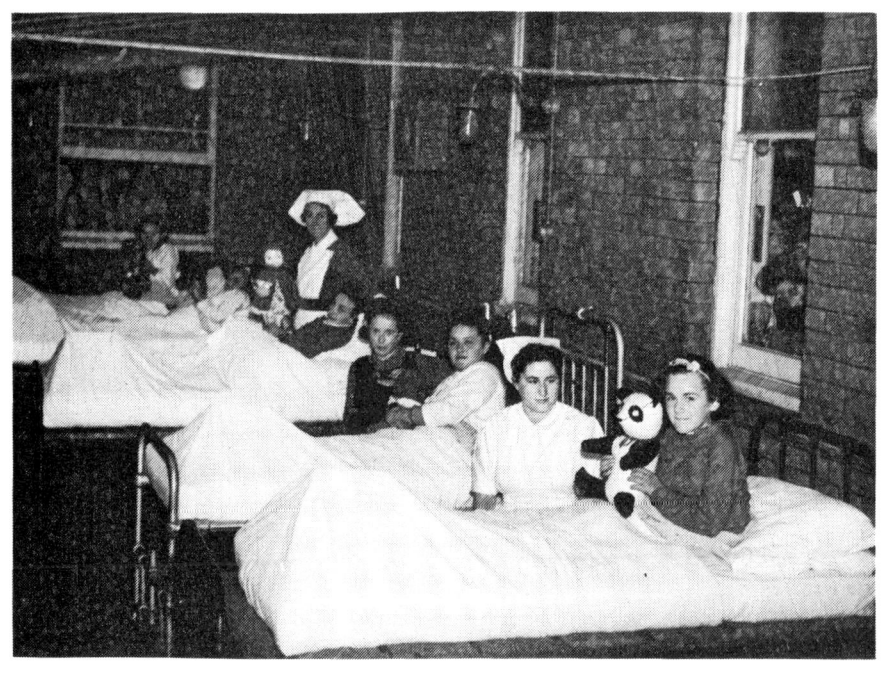

Post war late 40's early 50's single sex ward. Mixed wards came at the time of Dr. Lawson - end of the 50's

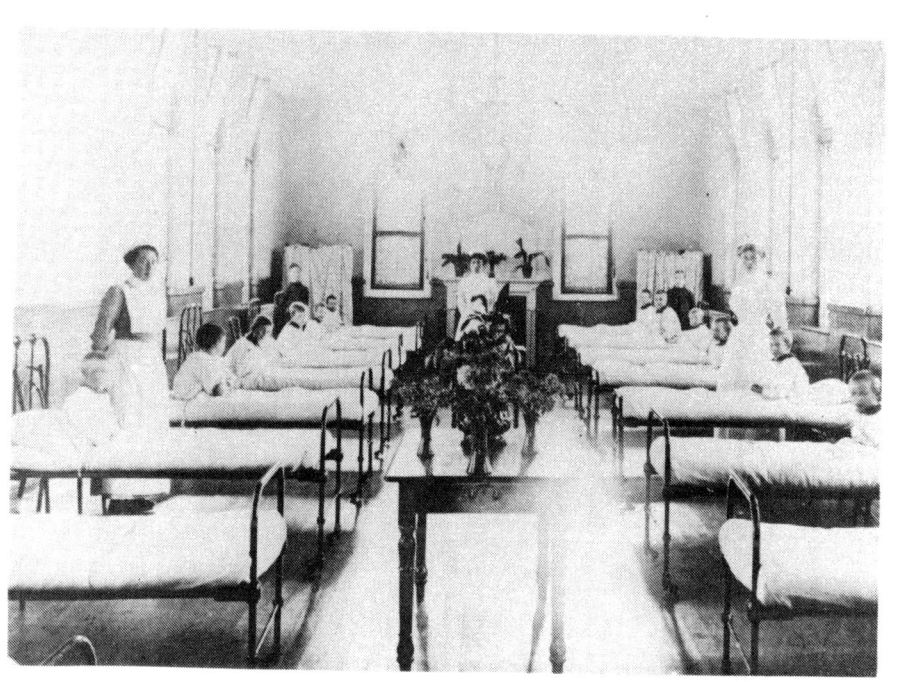

Group of nurses in 1933

Nurses in wartime uniform
(reproduced by kind permission of Nursing Times/Mirror)

Nursing staff nativity scene (former nursing tutor Muriel Hayman kneeling extreme left) (with the kind permission of the Nuring Times/ Mirror)

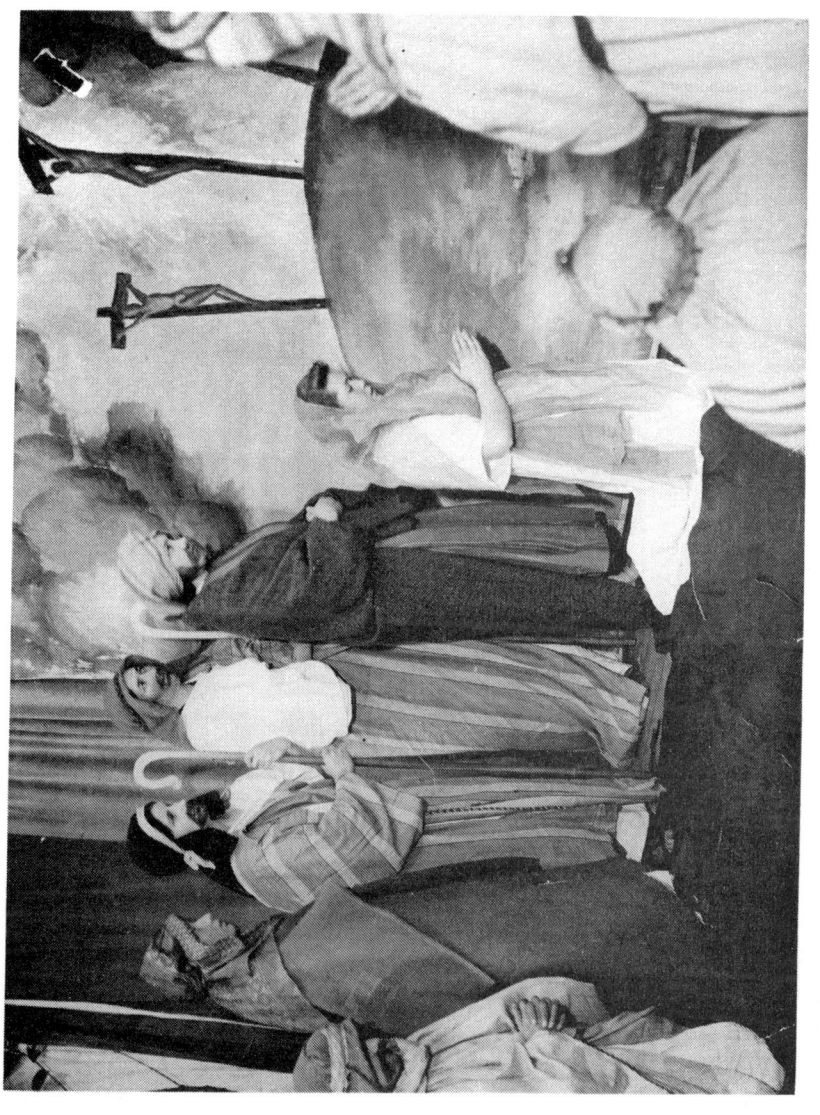

Nursing staff Easter play (with kind of permission of the Nursing Times/Mirror)

Wilfred Pickles visiting 1952

Special Church Service

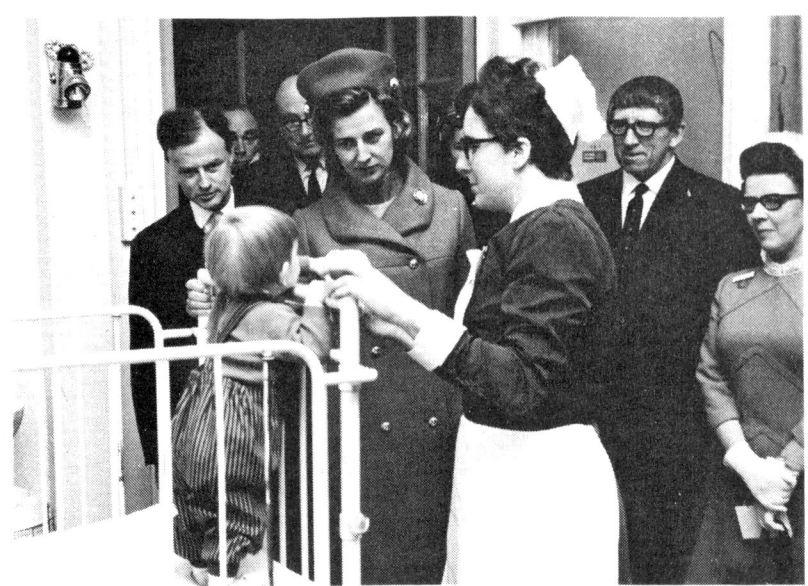

HRH Princess Alexandra visits the hospital. Extreme left Mr Eckstein on the right of the photograph Dr. Lawson and Sister Virginia Collis. Reproduced by kind permission of the Croydon Advertiser Group.

Sir Bobby Charlton visits the hospital.

Modern Times

Queen Mary's Staff

Mr Bill Annan JP

Bill was a Charge Nurse at Queen Mary's. He gained rapid promotion on completion of his nurse training due to his forward thinking and the innovations on his ward for people with learning disabilities.
At present Bill is a Magistrate, Branch Secretary and Staff Representative of the Staff Organisation at Orchard Hill. (Situated on the former Queen Mary's site).
His great concern has always been for the welfare of people with learning disabilities.

Consultant Paediatrician Dr. A.T. Piesowicz

L-R Ernie, Raphael and Dick(porters) Three Marathon Runners

Porters, Lee (left) and Ernie with head gardener Peter in the background.

The ever cheerful Derek on his dumper truck

Theatre staff   (L-R.)
Nurse Christine Renvoize, Dr. Guy Paremain, Nurse Barbara Watt

Long serving Queen Mary's Staff Nurse Julie Williams. A former member of the Hospital's athletic team, Julie is pictured here at Queen Mary's new location on the St. Helier site.

Staff Nurse Jenny doing the paperwork

A group of smiling nurses on Benjamin Bunny Ward
L-R Maureen, Tracy, Patsy and Sharon

The Last Post Registration Students at their exit bash 26th March 1993

L-R Marg, Gina, Rebecca and Rita at the party held by the PRSN's.

Saying farewell to Sister Snell (Stella) 14th May 1993

A group of staff at yet another farewell 13th July 1993

Children's Homecare team leader Greer Ramsammy-Westmaas being presented with a video recorder and alarms by the restricted members of Woodcote Park Golf Club following their charity fun day in 1993.

L-R Polly, Maggie (Theatre Sister) and Grace

Chris Taylor and Ernie the last two teachers on
Benjamin Bunny Ward (B3)

Reg Harman and Sheila Rutledge (Appliance Office) Reg was at the hospital for 33 years and retired when it closed on its original site.

Muriel Price driving Toby and Graham Hill driving Timmy from the Diamond Centre

In 1974 a very exciting event took place at Queen Mary's. Waved on by rows of cheering children and staff, HRH Princess Anne came through the hospital grounds to open the Diamond Riding Centre for Handicapped Riders.

A wonderful new concept that has brought joy to thousands of riders. Driving for the handicapped became an additional skill and the Diamond carriages were a regular sight in the hospital.

Scenes from the League of Friends Fete 1993

Sister Ryley (Alison) selling commemorative plates celebrating 80 years of caring

Two former Queen Mary's Sisters Margaret (left) and Julia

The train that goes round the hospital (not taken at fete)

The Jazz Band

Queen Mary's Buildings

The Old Style Entrance

The New Style Entrance

The Administration Block

Staff Residence

The Chapel

A3 Theatre

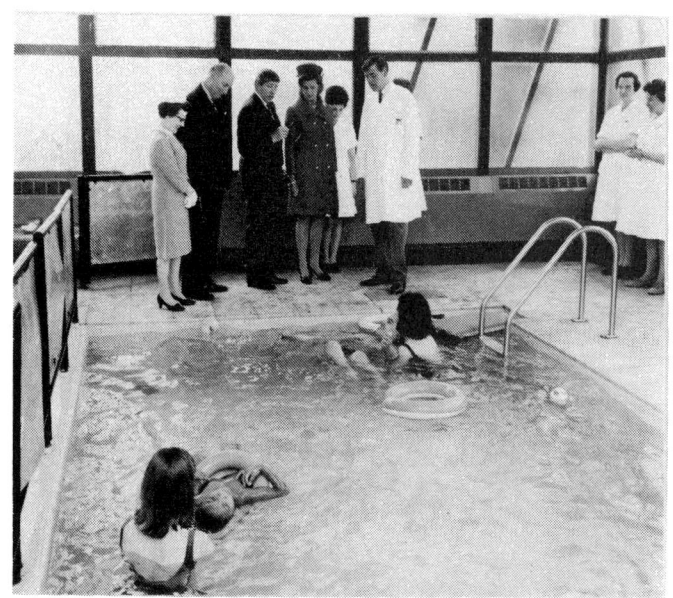

HRH Princess Alexandra on a visit to the heated indoor therapy pool built by Mr Pastry (Richard Hearn). On her right Dr. Lawson and on her left Mr Reynolds (superintendent physiotherapist) and Sister Virginia Collis.

The Fountain School opened by the worshipful Company of Drapers on 10th July 1968.

Queen Mary's Signs

The Entrance to the Drive

The Battery of Directions greeting the visitor

Alphabet Street, Badger Close, Caterpillar Walk

Formerly known as 'A' Street, 'B' Street, 'C' Street. These were the last 3 streets used by the children on the former Queen Mary's site.

Badger Close - showing the last ward open - Benjamin Bunny (B3)

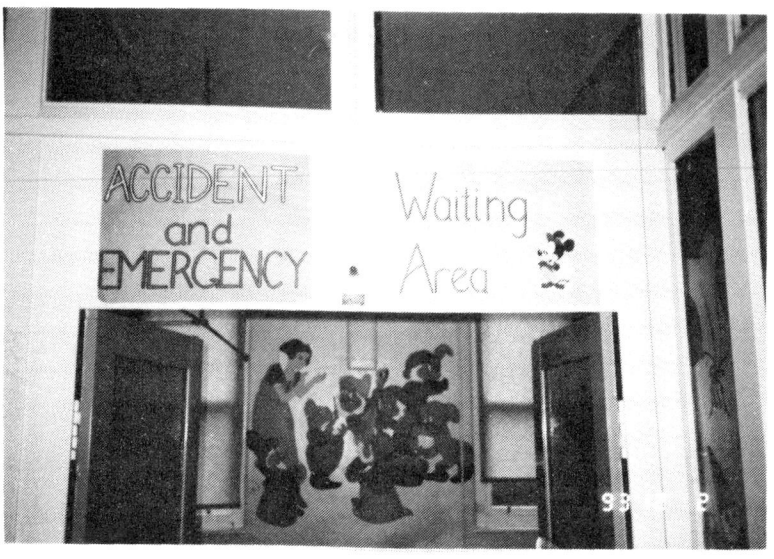

Accident and Emergency

The New Rainbow Centre

Last Day At Queen Mary's

Janice Ferguson - Nursing Officer

Dr. Harvey Williams (left) and Ernie

The ambulance crew - Kevin Longhurst, Matthew Durrant,
Reg Smith, Paul Meloy

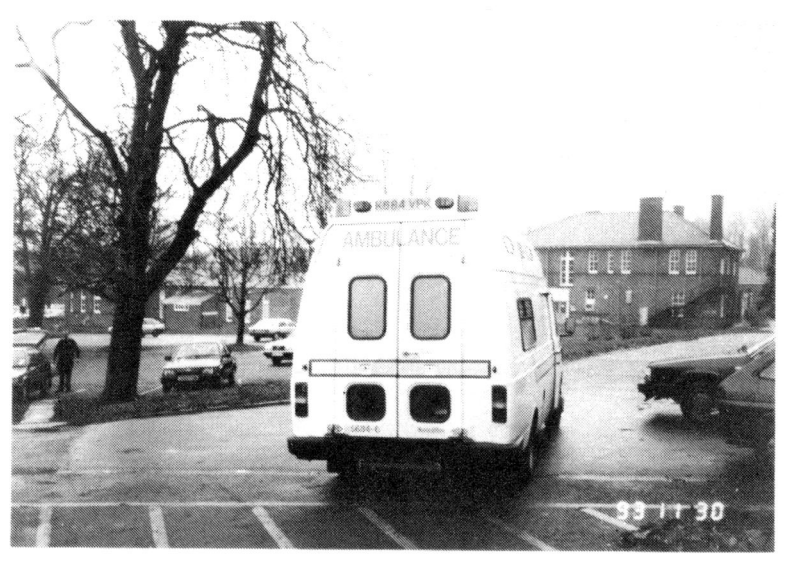

The ambulance taking the last patient to Leytonstone, London at 11.30 a.m.

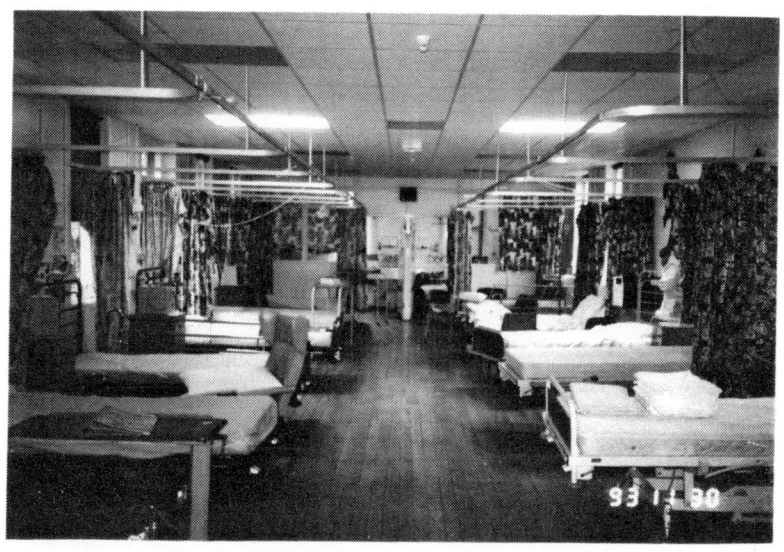

All the children have left 11.35 a.m.

The new sign at the Entrance to the drive

The Drive 4.30 p.m.

CHAPTER 9

HISTORY AND ARCHAEOLOGY

A BRIEF HISTORY OF QUEEN MARY'S HOSPITAL SITE

Kindly contributed by Mrs Margaret Cunningham, author of the book 'The Story of Little Woodcote and Woodcote Hall'.

The history of the land on which Queen Mary's Hospital was built commenced in prehistoric times. Its importance remained hidden for many centuries until work began on the hospital's foundations in 1903, when workmen digging a trench for drains at the southern end of the site dug through some black earth containing pottery and bones. Local archaeologists took the opportunity to carry out some investigations here until 1905 and, during this period, they found flint flakes and implements, charred grain and human bones. Also it was established that there had been an enclosed settlement here. Although it was impossible to assess the exact size of it and the extent of an outer ditch around it, partly due to erosion by the weather, and partly to constant ploughing of some of the land, it was estimated that it covered an area of about four acres.

A number of the flints and flakes uncovered on the site dated from the Mesolithic period (middle Stone Age c.7000 B.C.). Other flint implements found in and around the site were from the Neolithic period (late Stone Age c.4500 B.C.). Further archaeological investigations carried out from 1937 onwards have shown that the enclosed settlement was formed in the late Bronze Age (c.1200 - 700 B.C.) when, probably, it was of regional importance with control over ten kilometres across the surrounding downlands. The finds from this period included pottery, an amber bead, a ring with a suspension loop, perforated clay slabs, loomweights and spindle whorls, a flat, bronze fragment and a lump of copper, a bronze bar, a lancehead and a fragment of a bronze sword which was uncovered nearby in Little Woodcote. There were indications of both domestic and agricultural activities, including cattle and, possible, sheep-farming in and around the site. The finds of a large sherd of a bowl, some calcined flints, part of a bronze ingot and a piece of a possible crucible which were uncovered outside the earthworks suggested that this area was used for metal working.

Evidence of early Iron Age (700 - 500 B.C.) occupation of the site included some pottery and an important fragment of an urn or vessel from a source outside Britain. Also pottery dating from the late Iron Age (200 B.C. - 43 A.D.) probably indicated that this area was of some importance then. However, all of the finds did not necessarily substantiate the continuous occupation of the settlement from the Bronze Ages through to the late Iron Age.

The importance of the adjacent area of Woodcote in Roman times has been the subject of much speculation since the sixteenth century and up to present times. During the work on the hospital foundations in 1905, a small fragment of tile was found, and it resembled other Roman fragments. Roman pottery and coins have been discovered here as well. The hospital grounds have been suggested as a probable site for a Saxon cemetery after the discovery of pottery and burial urns dating from that period in history.

After the Norman Conquest and the introduction of the manorial system, the hospital's site was part of the southfields of Carshalton's manor that were used for agricultural purposes. The villagers were allowed to graze their cattle, sheep and horses in these fields at certain times of the year according to the rules laid down by the manorial Court, which also dealt out fines to anyone who disobeyed these laws.

The lordship of the manor passed through the hands of absentee owners until the mid-sixteenth century when it was held by **Henry Burton**. His great-grandson, Sir Henry, suffered severe financial losses as a royalist supporter before and during the beginning of the Civil War. He died in 1645 before the hostilities ceased and left his estate and debts to his younger brother, Charles, who sold some of the manorial lands to pay off his brother's mortgages and creditors. For the next fifty years, there was another succession of absentee lords of the manor until 1696, when the title passed to a rich merchant and financier, Sir William Scawen, who purchased the house called "Mascalls" and Carshalton Park previously owned by the Burtons. In 1712, he added the Barrow Hedges estate to his local properties. On his death in 1722, and because he had no children of his own, he left the bulk of his fortune and estates to his nephew, Thomas Scawen, who also bought up other parts of the original manor that had previously been divided into another moiety of it.An old deed relating to the Little Woodcote Estate provides evidence that, in 1751, Thomas's youngest brother, William Scawen, who was the owner of the Woodcote Lodge (now called Woodcote Hall in Wallington), leased some pieces of land that became part of the hospital's site from Sir Edward Stanley of Aldersley in Cheshire. Sir Edward was a kinsman of the Earls of Derby with the same family name of Stanley. He was entitled to these lands and others in the vicinity of them in the parishes of Carshalton and Beddington as the holder of a long-term lease for five hundred years dating from 10th January 1684. He had inherited it as a legatee named in the will of Dorothy Lenard, who was Anne Carew's sister and the residuary legatee named in Anne's will. The Carews of Beddington had held property in part of the manor of Carshalton since the early fifteenth century.

The same deed provides the information that other parts of the hospital's site belonged to Thomas Scawen's manor of Carshalton at that time. Also, Sir Edward Stanley's death had occurred before 1764 when William Scawen bought the lands he had leased from him from the widow, Dame Mary Stanley, her son, Sir John, and the executors of the deceased's will, and formed the Little Woodcote Estate.

Thomas Scawen died in February 1774 and left his large debts and estates to his only son, James, who also inherited Little Woodcote after the death of his uncle, William Scawen, in July 1775. Thus he became the owner of most of the lands on the hospital's site for the next twelve years. However, he was forced to sell off all of the properties he owned in order to pay off the monies owed by his late father.

The deed mentioned above shows that a good deal of the land on the eastern side of the hospital's site was sold in April 1787 to a local wealthy man, John Durand, when he purchased Little Woodcote and more lands from James Scawen's manor of Carshalton to form a larger Little Woodcote Estate. Meanwhile, the western side of the site had been bought by the next lord of the manor, George Taylor, in May 1786.

John Durand was a friend of the 12th Earl of Derby, who purchased The Oaks and 134 acres of the downlands around it from William Lambert in 1788. Previously the house and its grounds were leased successively by the 11th and 12th Earls of Derby since 1771. Mr. Durand died in July 1788 and Little Woodcote passed to his second eldest son, John Hodsdon Durand. He also was one of Lord Derby's hunting and racing friends. The Earl resided at The Oaks at the beginning of the nineteenth century whilst his house at Knowsley in Lancashire was altered and enlarged. He brought some of his stags and staghounds with him to enjoy stag-hunting across the local countryside. Young John Durand enjoyed this type of hunting very much and to commemorate it, he erected a large wooden tower with a gilt stag on top of it on part of the site of the Bronze Age enclosure, so that Lord Derby could see it from the rear windows of his mansion. The land around this "monument" was known as the "Stag Field" and its name was retained until it became part of the southern grounds of the hospital, although the tower had been taken down long before then.

In 1818, Mr. Durand sold the Little Woodcote Estate to another sporting gentleman, Mr. William Turner. On his death in 1829, it passed in trust to his six grandchildren but, by 1885, only Marcus and Montague Turner had survived to become the joint owners of their grandfather's property. They took out a mortgage for £80,000 on it and because the money was not repaid one year later as arranged, the Scottish Provident Institution, who were the mortgagees, became the Estate's new owners after they won the Court case against the Turner brothers.

The land on the western side of the hospital's site also had changed ownership. Carshalton's lord of the manor, George Taylor, died in 1814 leaving his properties to his brother, John, whose death occurred in 1832. His son, John, held them until 1664 when they were inherited by his son and heir, Captain William Taylor. Four years later, his young son, John, became the new owner of the estates while still a minor. By the time he came of age and took up an army career as a captain, the title of "lord of the manor" had become an anachronism. He sold the last of his 480 acres of land in 1895 and left the district. The eastern and western sides of the hospital's site were amalgamated in 1896 when both were purchased by the Metropolitan Asylums Board for the new hospital.

ECOLOGY AND PULSE

The first item kindly contributed by Sister Evelyn Upfold and former teacher Thelma Davidson. The remaining information is kindly contributed by Thelma.

* * * *

Each cluster of trees outside the wards is of a different and very special variety. At least five trees were planted to ensure continuity. One of the new bungalows narrowly escaped being hit by a fallen tree in the hurricane of 1987.

* * * *

There is a wonderful mulberry tree in the garden of the last house on the left as you come out of the porters lodge/office.

* * * *

The lane up to the old block was a haven for small blue butterflies, not rare but special. There were many foxes earths in front of ward D10.

* * * *

There was a regular school magazine called 'Pulse'.

SURREY ARCHAEOLOGICAL SOCIETY

REPORT ON EXCAVATIONS AT THE SITE OF THE EARLY IRON CAMP IN THE GROUNDS OF QUEEN MARY'S HOSPITAL, CARSHALTON, SURREY.

by
A W G Lowther, F.S.A.
reprinted by kind permission of the Surrey Archaeological Society

I. Discovery of Site

In 1903, when the foundations for the various buildings of Queen Mary's Hospital for Children were being dug, a silted-up ditch, containing a considerable quantity of Iron Age Pottery, was exposed in the foundations of several of the buildings. Two local archaeologists, Messrs. H C Collyer and N F Robarts, were present at the time and salvaged a quantity of pottery and subsequently cleared 20 yards of the ditch and published brief reports on the results (S.A.C., Vols XX (1907), XXII (1909); Trans. Croydon N. and S.S., 1906; and Journal of the Anthropological Institute, Vol. XXXV, pp. 387-97.

From these accounts, with which no plans or sections were published and only a few of the finds were illustrated, it was clear that a circular Iron Age Camp, about 500 feet in diameter had existed at the southern end of the hospital site. That a single ditch, of V-shaped section, 12 feet wide and 7 feet deep, had encircled a low hill (in what had been known as "Stag Field") which consisted of an "outlier" of Thanet sand resting on the chalk downland. No trace of a bank inside the ditch was found, but it was clear to the excavators that the loose sand had silted back into the ditch very rapidly and that, by Roman times, little trace of the earthwork can have existed. (These points were confirmed in the excavations here recorded).

The objects originally found were numerous and of various periods.

Flint implements, described as "Neolithic", a Bronze Age copper cake (apparently part of a founder's hoard); cylindrical loom-weights of late Bronze Age type; perforated tiles and pottery of Iron Age A, Iron Age C (Belgic) and Roman types. Only two vessels were figured (S.A.C., Vol. XX (1909), Pl. facing p.235 and consist of part of the rim and upper part of an urn of Belgic type (described as being of Aylesford type, but the fragment figured is insufficient to show what the lower part was like) and a small Iron Age biconical vessel with four handles. The latter vessel is to be compared with C1 and C9 of the present report.

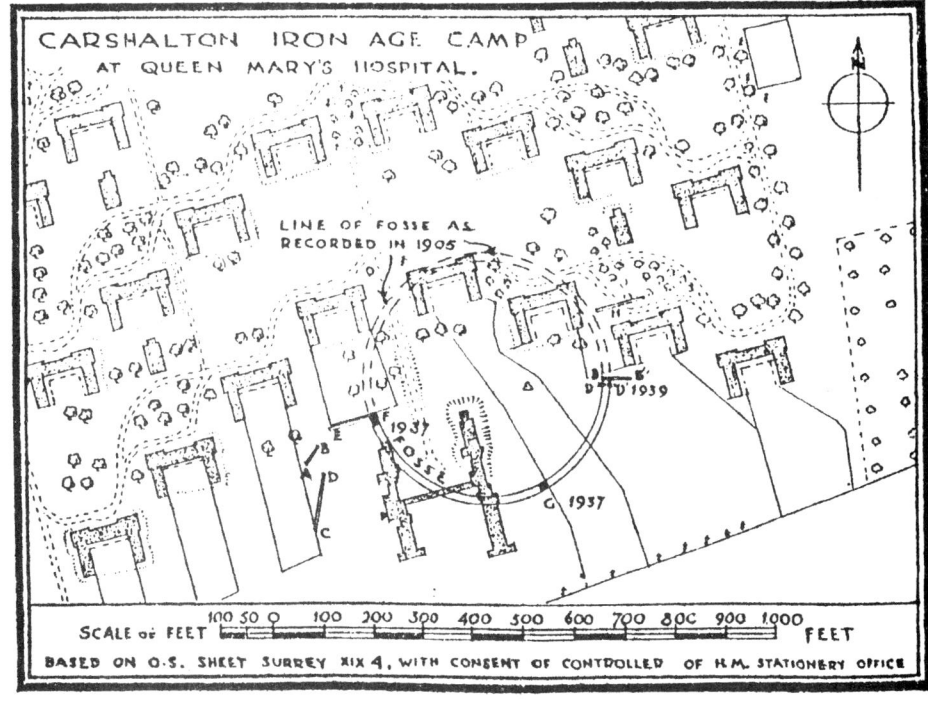

Fig. 1 Excavations at Carshalton; site plan

II. EXCAVATIONS

It was clearly desirable that some more precise information about this camp should be obtained and since at that time (1937) the late Sir Norman Grey Hull, who was himself very interested in the site, was on the staff of the hospital, it became possible for limited excavations to be undertaken. The expenses of this were were defrayed by the Surrey Archaeological Society, and a fortnight's excavation was carried out, under the writer's supervision, in 1937 and another fortnight's work in 1939, two labourers being employed on each occasion.

The first problem, in 1937, was that of locating the fosse, as there are no surface indications on the site and we had only the original accounts of the discovery as a guide. Two trenches (A-B and C-D on Plan, Fig.1) were dug before it was located at the east end of section E-F (Figs. 1 and 2). Here we were fortunate in finding it at a point where the ground had not been disturbed, just north of the west wing of the large Isolation block of the hospital. The section was drawn (Fig.2) and 20 feet length of the fosse excavated, a useful series of finds being obtained from each of the five levels of silt which filled it.

The fosse (Plate I,a,b) was found to be V-shaped, 14 feet wide at the existing lips and from 7 feet 3 inches to 7 feet 9 inches in depth below present surface. It has been excavated in firm, light-coloured Thanet sand. As was to be expected, the original ground slope had been steeper than that of the present surface and, while an original soil later (level 6) was present on the outer side of the fosse, it had disappeared on the inner side, nor was there any surviving trace of a vallum. Level 5 however, the "rapid silt" which, in view of the nature of the subsoil, must have washed back into the fosse extremely rapidly, shows a thickening on the east (inner) side on which the vallum can be presumed. Well down in level 5 were found almost all the fragments of a wide-mouthed bowl (C2) of a well defined Iron Age A type (discussed later, in the description of the finds). The skull of a dog was also found in this level.

Level 4, consisting of chalk speckled sand, contained, particularly at the bottom, many large flints and several blocks of chalk. It seems probable that these had been used to revet the face of the inside of the vallum and retain the sand excavated when the fosse was dug.

Plate 1

a

b

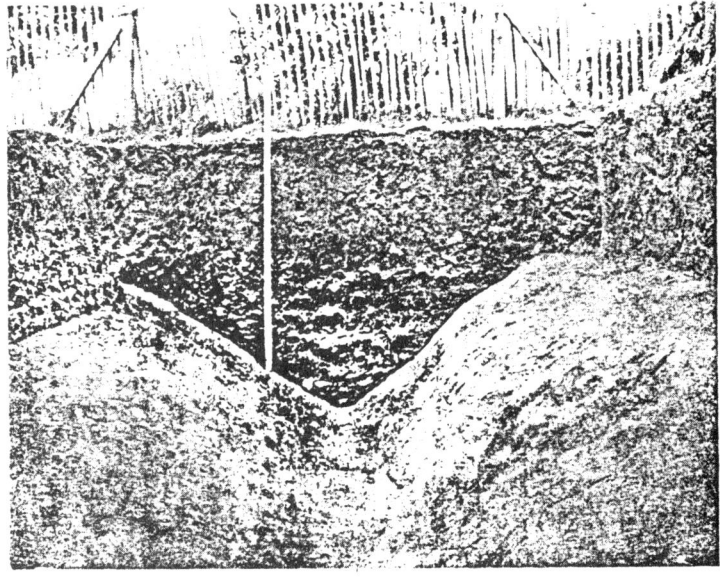

174

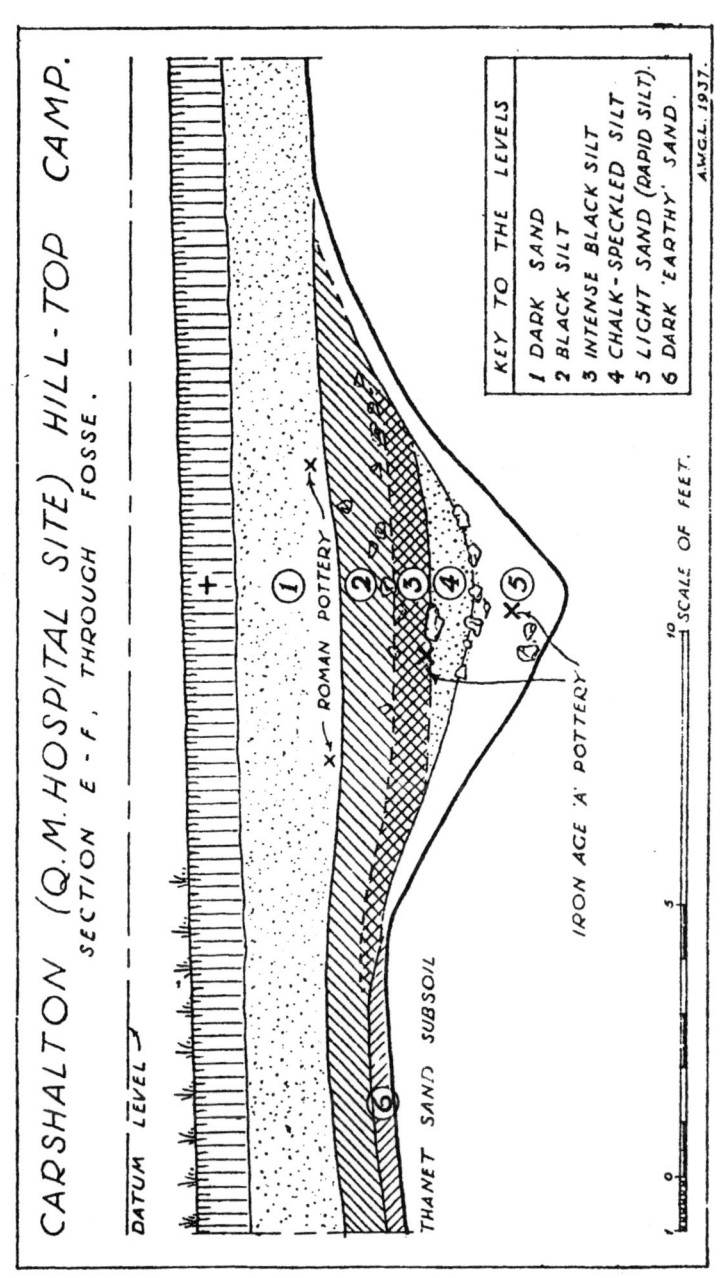

Fig.2 - Excavations at Carshalton : Section through fosse E-F

Level 3, most prolific in finds, was a layer of intensely black, charcoal-impregnated sand, containing animal bones, calcined flints, and the vessels C3 and C5 which are both characteristic Iron Age pots of highly burnished black ware.

Level 2, only differentiated from level 3 in not being so black, contained more Iron Age A pottery, fragments of saddle querns and flint flakes and implements.

A well-defined line, probably an original turf line, separated the dark-brown sandy silt of level 1 from level 2. Several fragments of Iron Age C pottery were found in level 1, also a small fragment of a bronze implement, apparently part of an axe (see Fig.10). (A piece of bronze ingot had previously been found in the western end of the trench E-F, in the continuation of this same level).

Level 1, hill-wash consisting of slightly earthy sand, was clearly formed from Roman times onwards. An interesting point was that it contained, in addition to the two bronze fragments just referred to, numerous fragments of late Bronze Age ware and several flint scrapers of Bronze Age type. It thus appeared that there had been some Late Bronze Age occupation on or near the top of the hill within the limits of the succeeding Iron Age A Camp, (Two Mesolithic cores and a few implements of Neolithic type were also from this level).

Apart from a small hollow which contained the shard of the vessel C4 and some calcined flints, found in trench A-B, trenches A-B and C-D yielded no results. The remaining trench dug in 1937 (at G on Plan) was with the object of verifying the line of the fosse where it was known to have been found in 1903. This it accomplished, and the filling had clearly all been disturbed recently though it contained a quantity of pot sherds and the filling was all of an intensely black nature (verifying the great contents of occupation debris noted by the previous excavators as being most intense in this southern sector).

The 1939 excavations (Fig.3) were (within the limits of where it was permissible to excavate) directed towards locating the fosse on the eastern side of the camp. Here, contrary to expectations, an entirely different state of affairs was found to have existed. Three trenches were dug, but only in one (section D-D) was the inner side of the fosse located. This was due

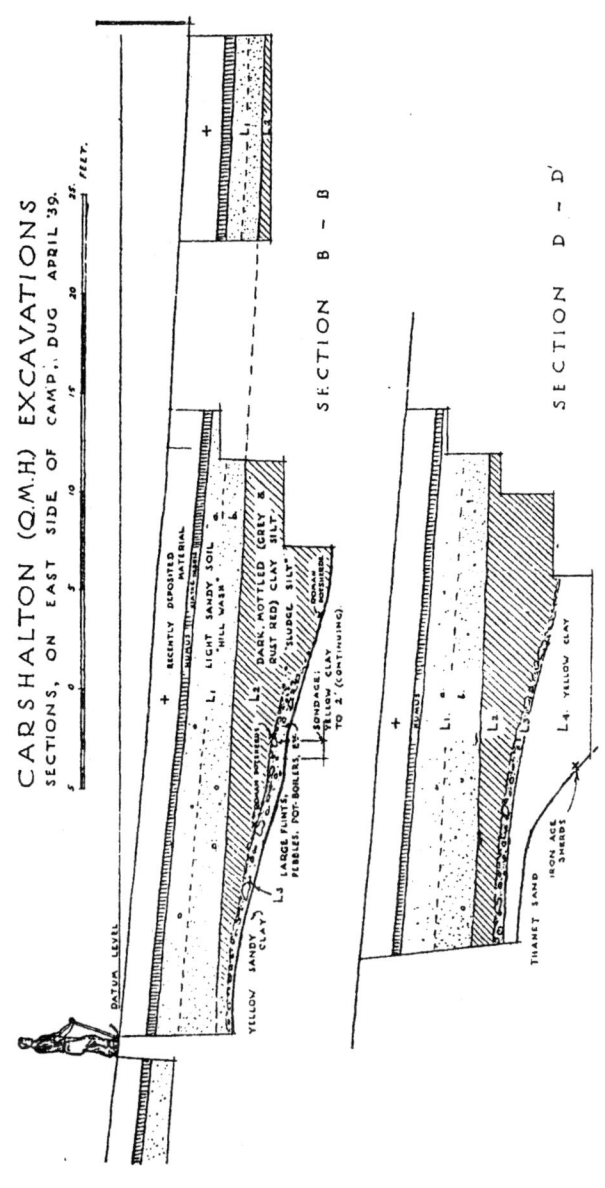

Fig 3 Sections at east side of camp

to the greater depth of overlying material, so that it was only at the end of the time available that we realised that it was necessary to go deeper, through the yellow clay (level 4) which in trench B-B had been taken for an undisturbed natural deposit. Also, as will shortly be described, a heavy clay silt (level 2) had to be penetrated before reaching the Roman level. In addition, some 2 feet of recently deposited material encumbered the surface of the site.

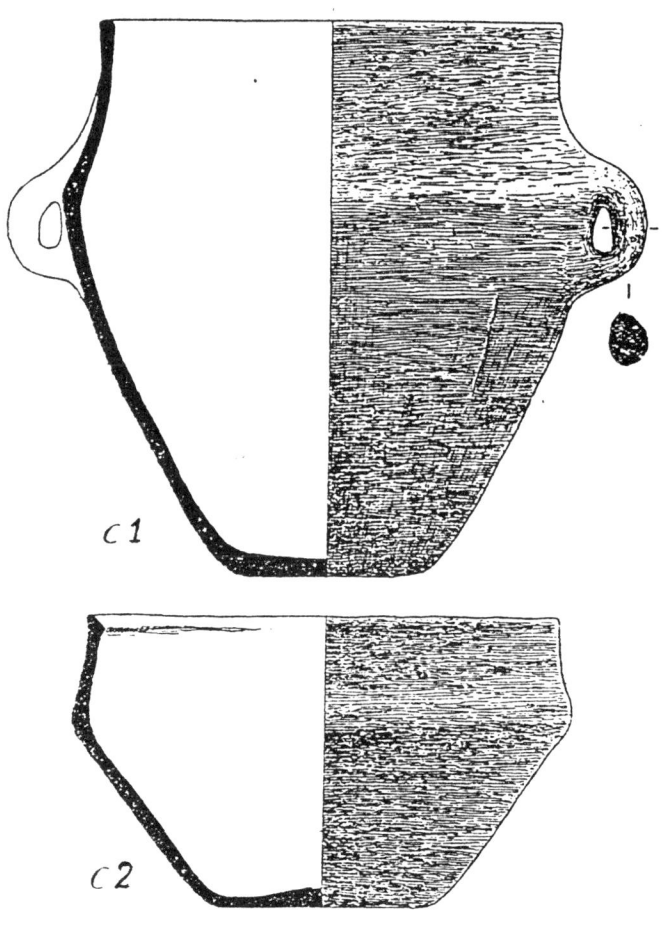

Fig. 4 Handled jar and bowl

Level 1, divisible into layers "a" and "b" through the lower layer containing rather more pebbles but otherwise uniform, was found to rest on a dark, red-brown and grey, mottled sandy clay (level 2) containing small water-worn sherds of Roman and Iron Age ware, pieces of saddle quern, worked flakes and a certain number of calcined flints. It was clearly a water-laid deposit such as would form in marsh or pond and the rusty streaks seem to be the product of vegetation, such as reeds.

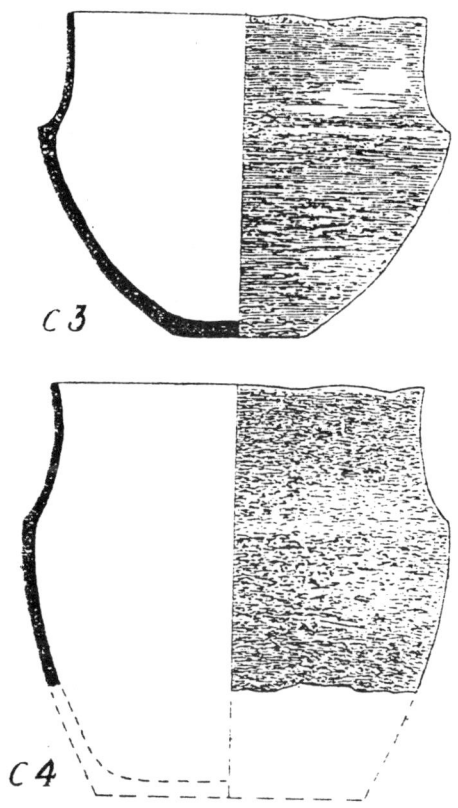

Fig. 5 Two jars : Iron age A

Level 3 was a gravel and large flint layer, and contained the pieces of Roman pot (at a depth of 7 feet 6 inches) shown on Fig.9. This is not likely to be earlier than the end of the 1st century A.D. A sounding, made to a depth of 2 feet into the yellow clay (level 4) of Section D-D) failed to reveal anything to suggest it was not an undisturbed deposit, but in Section D-D several scraps of Iron Age pottery and particles of charcoal were found in it and on what was clearly the inner slope of the fosse, when eventually this was reached. It is to be regretted that a full section of the fosse was not obtained, but the excavation which would have been involved could not then be undertaken.

III. THE FINDS
A. Pottery
(i) Bronze Age. Of the late Bronze Age sherds found, only one (Fig. 7. C14) is worthy of illustration. This is a piece, from a short distance below the rim, of a large jar with cable ornament round the neck. It can be paralleled by similar pieces from the Late Bronze Age site at Scarborough, Yorks (R.E.M. Wheeler, History of Scarborough, Scarborough, 1931; also T.D. Kendrick and C.F.C. Hawkes, Archaeology in England and Wales, 1914-31, London 1932 p.151, Fig. 60, Nos. 10, 11 and 12).

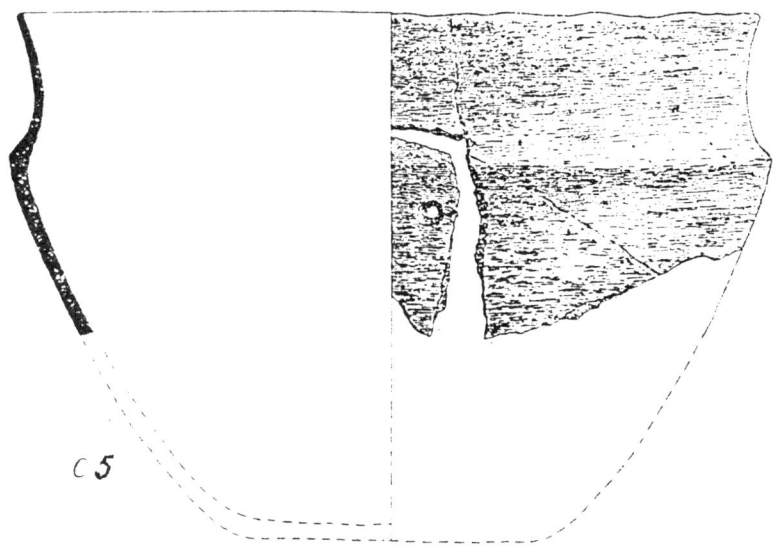

Fig. 6 Fragments of jar : Iron age A

(ii) Iron Age A. (Vessels C1-C5 have been restored and are now in Guildford Museum).

Plate II

**Carshalton Iron age camp: Pottery (restored) from Fosse at E-F
a(C1) b(C3) and c (C2)**

C1 (Plate II a.Fig.4). Handled jar, of brown to black smooth-surfaced ware. A somewhat similar vessel from Maiden Castle, Dorset, is illustrated on Fig. 60, No. 70, of the Report. From E-F, level 2. Also with this vessel should be compared C9 (Fig.7.), a smaller vessel of similar type, and that illustrated in the original report S.A.C. Vol.XX, which is still smaller (4 $^1/_2$ inches in height, and 2 inches rim diameter) and has four loop-shaped handles.

C2 (Plate II c.Fig.4). Bowl, of similar ware to the last, from the rapid silt of E-F, level 5. This must have reached its position in the ditch within a matter of a few weeks of the latter being dug, and therefore is of the utmost importance for fixing the date of the camp. A very similar bowl, found at the Trundle (Goodwood, Sussex) is figured by Dr.Curwen who describes it as belonging to his A2 series of circa 250-100 B.C.

C3 (Plate II b. Fig.5) and C5 (Fig.6). Vessels of very black ware with highly burnished outer surface. Found together in E-F, level 3. One fragment of C5 is perforated after make, apparently for a repair thong or rivet.

C4 (Fig.5). Shouldered pot of dark brown ware found, as previously described, outside the camp in section A-B.

The remainder of the pottery figured (Fig.7, C6-C14) was found in level 2 of section E-F, mainly at the bottom of the layer.

C6 is the only fragment found with "pie-crust" ornament on the rim, though several pieces from the disturbed material in trench G had "finger-nail" ornament along the top of the rim, so it is clear that ornamented ware was not absent from this site.

C13 is one of two pot bases found which had been perforated, subsequent to manufacture. Iron Age pots similarly perforated have frequently been found, but their purpose is not clear.

(iii) Haematite-surfaced ware (not figured). Two small pieces of ware with thick deep-red haematite coating on the exterior (from E-F, level 2, and B-B level 2) were found during the excavations. That from E-F is of light grey ware and the haematite coating had originally been highly burnished; that from B-B is of darker grey ware containing, unlike the other, particles of flint grit. It is somewhat water-worn, so has lost its original surface, but the coating is also of considerable thickness. Haematite ware has been the subject of several recent articles, as its distribution, is a matter of considerable importance in assessing the origins, distribution and trading contacts of the Iron Age people who produced it. It is clear that the main centre where this pottery was produced was in Wessex midway between the Isle of Wight and the Severn and that it spread, either by trade or folk movement, along the north and south downs into Surrey and Sussex and hence (possibly by sea, as there is a hiatus in sites where it has been found) to the extreme east of Kent.

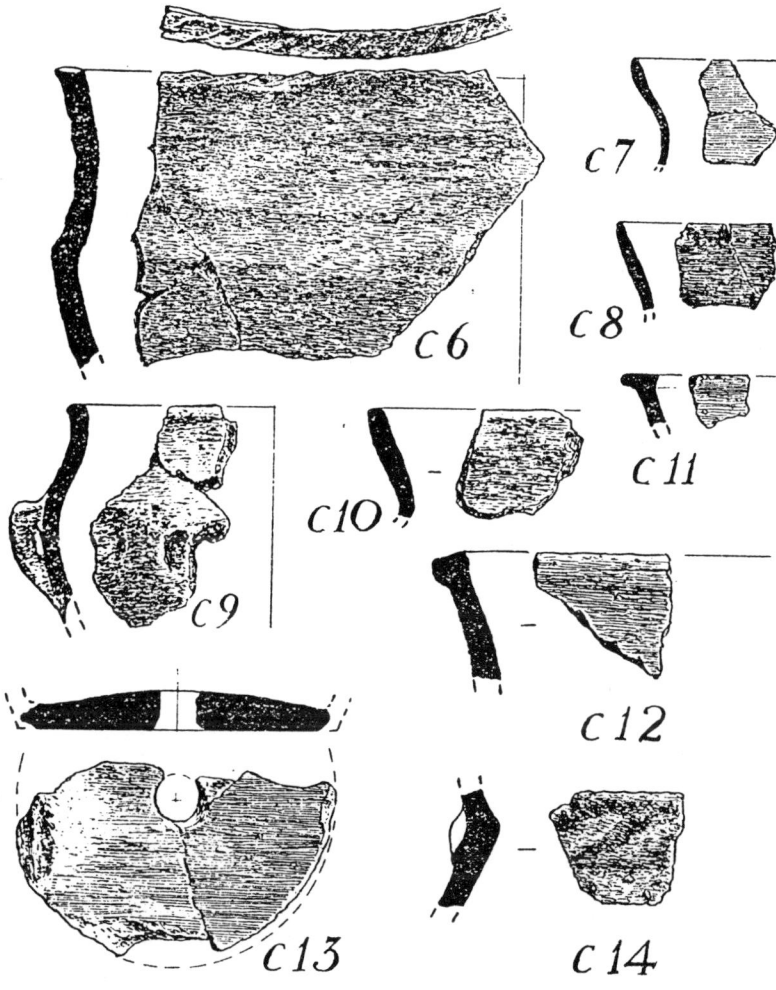

Fig. 7 Fragments of pottery

In connection with the Carshalton pieces, it seems clear that they are imports to the site, probably by trade, since only the two small fragments were found. The one with light-coloured gritless pottery is similar to the pieces of this ware found at Margate (now in the B.M.), while the other is like the fragments found by Mr Frere at Epsom. Neither piece gives any information as to the form of the vessels to which they belonged.

Surrey sites at which analogous pottery has been found (Map, Fig.8).

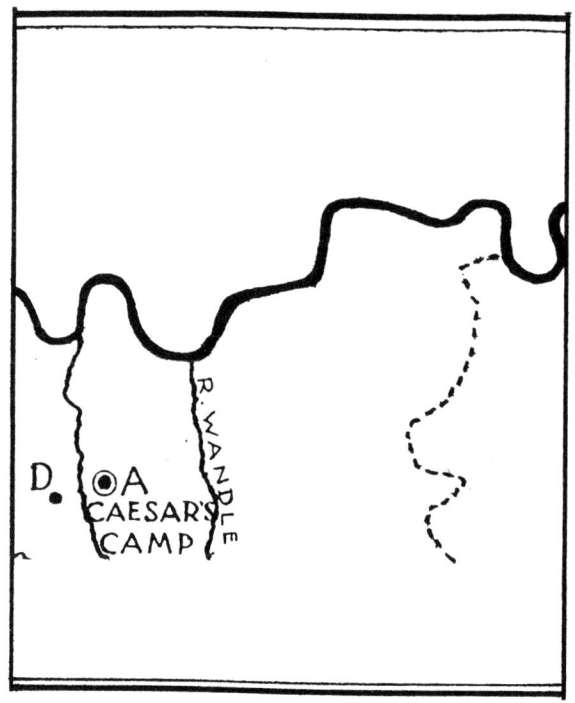

As regarded the relation of the Iron Age pottery from this site/to that from other Surrey Iron Age sites, this is being dealt with in a paper on all Surrey Iron Age sites which the writer has in preparation, and hopes to be have published at a later date. Here it is only possible to refer briefly to the main analogies.

1. "Caesar's Camp" Wimbledon Common (A). This Camp, which in its form (single bank and ditch and circular plan) bears a close resemblance to the one at Carshalton, had a trench dug through it in 1937 for the laying of a water main. The excavations were supervised by the writer and Mr F Cottrill, and are the subject of a report now in preparation, appearing in Arch. Journ., Vol. CII. Pottery found in a shallow pit, inside the vallum on the east side of the camp, is similar to much of that from Carshalton, but also includes vessels with "finger-tip" ornament applied to rim and, round the sides, along the bulge line.

2. Epsom (near Epsom College) op.cit.(R) produced several analogous sherds, including two with "pie-crust" ornament, similar to C6.

3. Ewell-(a). Garden of "Purberry Shot" (not yet published) (F). Includes fragments, of form C4 and C5, of burnished, shouldered bowls with upstanding rims as well as vessels with finger-tip ornament as from Wimbledon.

(b) A site in Nonsuch Park, on the west side of Ewell, still to be published (E).

Other Surrey sites which have produced pottery of similar types are:-

4. Coombe Warren, Kingston Hill (Kingston Museum; mainly unpublished) (D)

5. Cobham, Leigh Hill, (S.A.C., Vol.XXI,i) (B)

6. Fetcham, Hawk's Hill (S.A.C., Vol.XX) (H)

7. Ashstead, garden of "Inward Shaw" (S.A.C., forth-coming) (G)

8. Wisley (Proc.Prehist.Soc.,1945,pp.32-38) (I)

9. Guildford (a) St.Catherine's Hill (S.A.C.,forth-coming; Arch.Journ.Vol.CII) (K)

10. Farnham, Shortheath Ridge (S.A.S., Preh.Farnh.) (S)

Many of these sites have, in addition, produced pottery of later Iron Age types, but with which the present paper is not concerned.

(IV) Roman Pottery (Fig.9) Pieces of three vessels were found in level 3 of section B-B (Fig.3) The two figured are:-

1. Upper part of a small pot of brown ware, with black, fumed, inner and outer surfaces (C15. max. diam. 5 1/2 inches).

2. Piece of jar rim of grey ware. (C16.diam. 4 1/2 inches).

3. (Not figured) Fragments from the body of a small flagon. Grey ware with red outer surface.

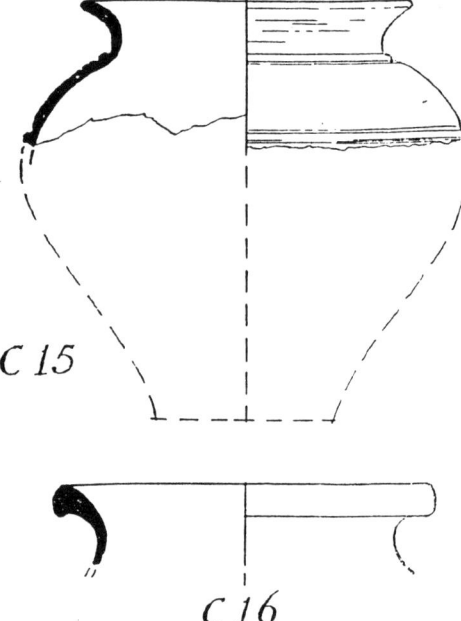

All three can be dated c. A.D. 90-100, and are similar to vessels of this period found at the Roman villa on Ashstead Common.

B. Bronze Axe (Fig.10)

The fragment, possible part of a flat axe and, if so, of Early Bronze Age date, has apparently been deliberately broken and therefore, with the additional evidence of the pieces of ingots found nearby, one may presume that a "founder's hoard" once existed on this site and became scattered during the subsequent occupation.

Fig. 9 Roman pottery from B-B level 3

Several other hoards have been found in the vicinity, the nearest in the railway cutting only about two miles north of this site, and others at Beddington on the River Wandle, at Croydon and Banstead, but all of late Bronze Age date and including socketed axes. It is possible that the present fragment is actually from a socketed axe; it is too small for any certainty.

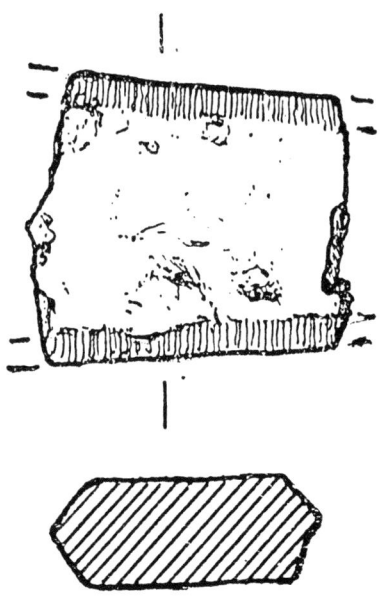

Fig.10 Fragment of Bronze axe

C. Saddle Querns

One complete saddle quern (10 inches by 6 1/2 inches by 2 inches), oval in shape) was found in B-B level 2 and the pieces of several others. All except one are of similar stone, a gritty sand-stone of greenish-brown colour, possibly from the greensand outcrop several miles to the south (an expert opinion on the stone has still to be obtained). The exception just referred to is made of sarsen stone and, possibly owing to the nature of this material, is of different type from the remainder (Fig. 15). As the unabraded under- and edge-surfaces show, it was formed by "pecking", producing a finely pitted surface. It was (as this softish, fine-grained sandstone allowed) carefully sloped with a straight vertical edge and true bevel of the under angle. The upper surface, probably as a result of wear during use, dishes towards the centre, and has in part, acquired a high polish. The stone, of a silvery white colour, full of small particles which glitter in strong light, has its outer surface stained a red-brown colour from the clay silt (level 2 of section B-B) in which it was found.

Fragments of identical querns have been found at sites in Croydon, Ashstead and Thorpe.

As regards the provenance of this stone (which is derived from the geological deposits of the Upper Tertiaries known as the Barton Beds) this is likely to have been in the neighbourhood of Aldershot, at Fox Hills and the Chobham Ridges, where deposits of sarsen stone are still more or less in situ (The Geology of the Country around Aldershot and Guildford, Memoirs of the Geological Survey of England and Wales, No. 285, p. 102). It seems reasonable to suppose that querns of this stone were made in this westernmost region of Surrey and reach eastern Surrey through trade, thus emphasising the east to west trackway (the so-called Harroway) of which the Hog's Back ridgeway, between Guildford and Farnham, formed a part (See S.A.S. Prehist. Farnh.)

D. Loom-weights

Several loom-weights, of vertically-perforated cylindrical type, were found in 1903 and the worn fragment of another in 1937. The latter was from a disturbed level. It seems likely that these belong to the Late Bronze Age occupation at this site, already referred to. Triangular loom-weights of normal Iron Age A type (as found with pottery of this date at St. Martha's

Hill, near Guildford, S.A.C., Vol. SLIII (1935), Pl. XIII) were not found during the present excavation.

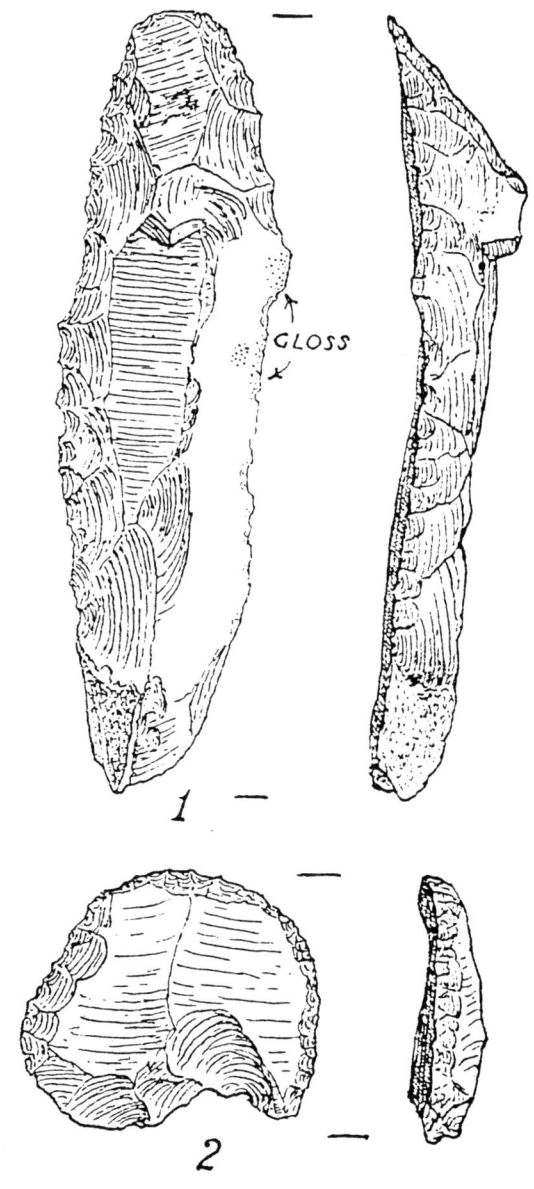

Fig 11 Sickle-Flint and scraper from E-F Level 1

E. Flints (Figs. 11-14)

As previously stated, worked flints (scrapers, cores and numerous flakes) were found at all levels in the ditch, but in greatest quantity in the hill-wash sand (level 1) of section E-F.

These include two cores (Fig.12) of typical, double-ended Mesolithic form.

No.1 (Fig.11) A sickle flint (with traces of "corn glass" on one edge) of grey flint with considerable secondary flaking along the steep side and round the end, and with a piece of cortex remaining at the butt end. Length, 5 5/8 inches. Neolithic or Early Bronze Age (?) From E-F, level 1.

Also of this period, and of similar light grey, mottled flint, is the broad scraper, No.2 (Fig.11). (Several flakes, of identical flint, are likely to belong to the period of these two implements).

The remainder of the implements, all of black or brown flint with some grey mottling, are possible of Bronze Age date. Most retain some cortex, coloured light brown on the surface but showing the thick, white underlying crust where exposed by flaking. Two of them are end scrapers, with cortex remaining down one side, and one flake, shows fine ripple-flaking extending along one edge on alternate faces, but the specimen has been fractured at a subsequent date. Two single-platform cores, retaining much cortex, are clearly contemporary with the scrapers and bear flake scars from which similar pieces have been detached.

The following observations on the flint implements have been contributed by Mr W.F. Rankine, F.S.A. Scot.

"Material: Grey porous flint with cherty patches and sporadic groups of pyrites; longitudinally runs a blue-grey band (5mm) containing globular organic inclusions, and this may explain the porosity of the surrounding flint; there is a fossil bivalve on under surface. Bulbar extremity of the implement is fire-crackled".

Mr Rankine is of opinion that the implement is a "crude backed knife". Dr. Curwen endorses the writer's suggestion that it is a sickle flint, and probably hafted at the bulbar end, with the possibility that the fire-crackling at this end is due to burning of the wooden haft.

2. (Fig.11) "Mesolithic scraper of grey flint with bluish mottling. A heavy scraper- bulb removed".

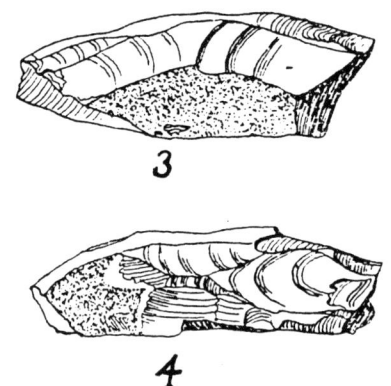

Fig.12 Mesolithic cores

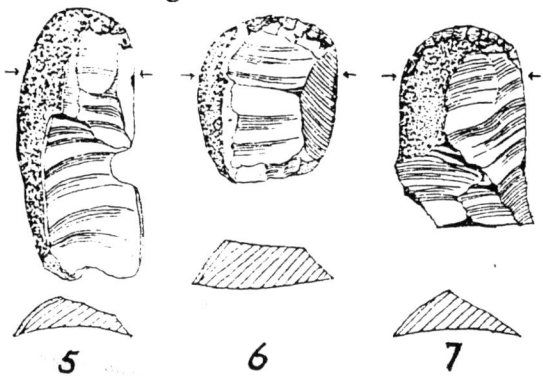

Fig.13 End Scrapers

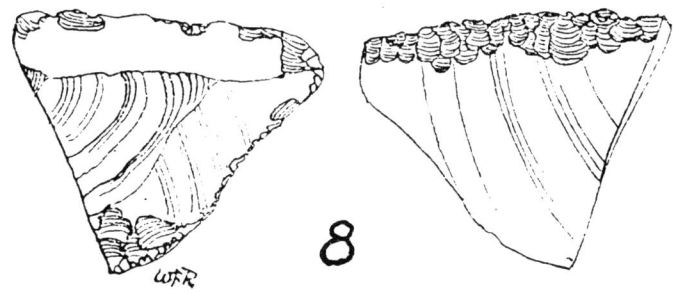

Fig. 14 Part of Arrow-Head

3 and 4 (Fig.12). "Mesolithic cores. No.2 is a fresh specimen. Colour rather remarkable for this type (i.e Mesolithic). In West Surrey brown colour (due to sand and chemical content) mainly that of Neolithic - Bronze Age period flints.

5, 6 and 7 (Fig.13). "End scrapers - one debulbed. No.6 practically a round scraper. Colour as last".

8 (Fig.14) "Part of an arrow-head of petit tranchet derivative type".

The low, sand-capped hill to the south of Queen Mary's Hospital, Carshalton, was the scene of some occupation in Mesolithic, Early Bronze Age and Late Bronze Age times (and, possibly, also in the Neolithic period). In the Iron Age (A2) period there was considerable occupation, and at this time the summit of the hill was encircled by defences consisting of a single ditch and mound. There is no evidence to show the position of the entrance (or entrances) but it is suspected that one existed at the point now crossed by the connecting corridor of the Isolation building in the southern sector of the camp.

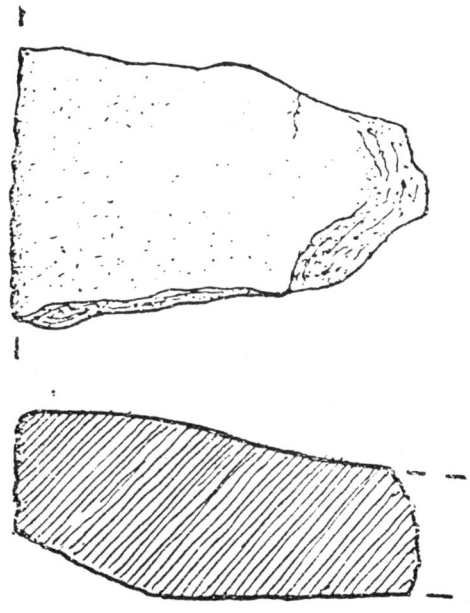

Fig.15 Fragment of Quern of Sarsen stone

There was, apparently some Belgic occupation nearby (attested by a few stray sherds) but by this time the mound had silted, or been ploughed, back into the ditch and there can have been little trace of it on the surface.

Except on the eastern side where a marsh or pool seems to have formed (helped by the presence of Reading clay in this part of the Tertiary outlier) most of the site, and the surrounding chalk downland, was probably being cultivated in Roman times and the scatter of Roman pottery (and one piece of flanged roof tile) indicates no extensive occupation in this area.

Appendix.

Report on the animal bones from the fosse, Section Y, by Dr. J Wilfred Jackson, D.Sc., F.G.S., F.S.A.

From level 3:-

Horse - Three incisor teeth and an ulna. The latter is small and has a full length of about 305mm. The animal appears to have been small in size of the Exmoor pony type, of 11 1/2 to 12 1/2 hands in height, as in other Iron Age sites.

Pig - Imperfect ulna.

Sheep - Maxilla with three teeth, and fragmentary limb-bones, including a young shank-bone.

Ox - Fragmentary horn cores of the Celtic ox type, one molar, calcaneum 120mm. long, head of humerus, proximal half of radius, imperfect tibia about 300 mm. long and part of a young tibia. The bones indicate small animals similar to the Kerry cattle.

From level 5:-

Dog - Axis vertebra fragments of skull, fragment of maxilla with two teeth, premaxillae with no teeth, left ramus of mandible with canine and incisor. In the latter the length of the tooth-row (teeth missing) is 78 mm. The remains are too fragmentary for the determination of type, but they agree with similar ones from other Iron Age sites.

CHAPTER 10

CONCLUSION

I can think of no better conclusion to this book than the following poem written by Jennifer Buckell.

**In Loving Memory of
'Queen Mary's Hospital for Children'**

It stood there like a flower
Calmly, slowly and beautifully growing.
And the people there changed as the years went by
Like clouds gliding across the sky.
This place was old and wise,
You could never feel out of place.
What ever they do to the building of art and love,
They could never take away its ghost,
And the distant laughter of the children.
And they could never take away the presence
Of the magnificent people who worked there
From us, the people.

Jenny Buckell
(Spinal Fusion, December 1990).

Researching this book has proved to be a most interesting excercise. The more that I have unearthed the more I have discovered just how much of the Queen Mary's story remains untold. **A Sequel?**

Let all who are privileged to know Queen Mary's Hospital for Children carry the memory within their hearts and souls and thank
God for them all.

Queen Mary's Badges